PRACTICAL
CAKE DECORATING
TECHNIQUES

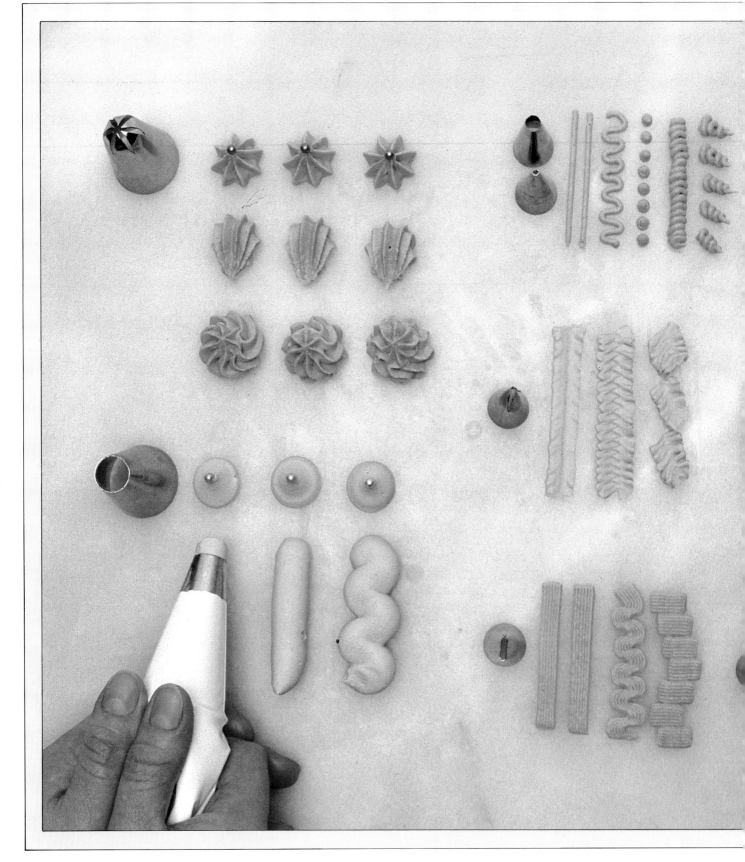

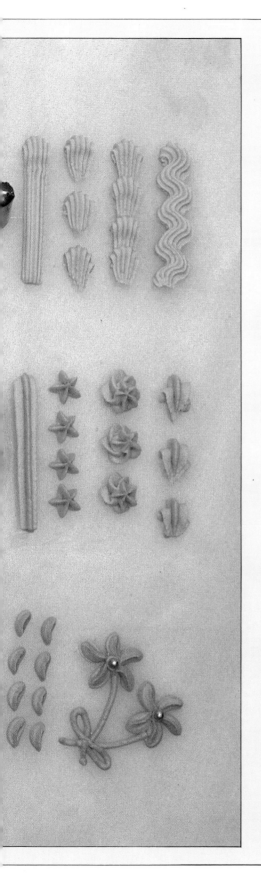

PRACTICAL
CAKE DECORATING
TECHNIQUES

EDITED BY EMMA CALLERY

TIGER BOOKS INTERNATIONAL
LONDON

A QUINTET BOOK

This edition first published in 1991 by
Tiger Books International PLC
London

This book was designed and produced by
Quintet Publishing Limited
6 Blundell Street
London N7 9BH

Designer: Carole Perks
Photographers: David Burch, Zul Mukhida,
James Stewart, John Heseltine
Project Editor: Emma Callery
Editor: Laura Sandelson

Typeset in Great Britain by
En to En Typesetters, Tunbridge Wells
Manufactured in Singapore by
Chroma Graphics (Overseas) PTE. LTD.
Printed in Spain by
Gráficas Estella, S.A.

The material in this publication previously
appeared in *Step-by-Step Cake Decorating, Cake
Making and Decorating* and *Cake Decorating*.

Contents

Chapter One:
EQUIPMENT AND BASIC RECIPES

*Successful cake decorating relies on successful cake making.
There is no point in spending hours elaborately decorating a
cake that has not been properly baked. By following a few
simple rules and using a good recipe, you can ensure a good
result every time. It is particularly important to know your oven
and make any minor adjustments to baking times and
temperatures that are necessary.*

*This section gives advice on equipment, preparing cake pans,
cooling, storing and freezing cakes, and how to test whether your
cake is cooked and avoid common baking mistakes.*

*Some basic recipes are also given in this section and these are the
cakes used for decoration in the following sections of the book.
You may have your own tried and tested recipes and you can, of
course, use these instead.*

BASIC EQUIPMENT

Hand-held electric mixer

*Kitchen scissors.
A smaller pair is
also useful for more
intricate cutting*

Balloon whisk

*Palette knives — 13cm/5in and
18cm/7in are the two most
useful sizes*

Skewer

A set of measuring spoons

*A selction of kitchen papers, which should include greaseproof
or waxed paper, non-stick paper, cling film and aluminium foil*

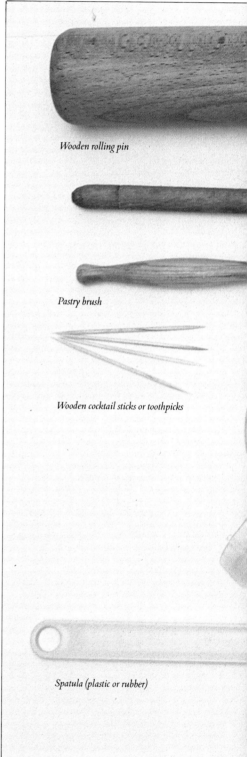

Wooden rolling pin

Pastry brush

Wooden cocktail sticks or toothpicks

Spatula (plastic or rubber)

String

A selection of wooden and metal spoons

Sieve — 15cm/6in size is the most useful

Measuring jug

A selection of mixing bowls, preferably glass or china

SPECIAL EQUIPMENT

Most of the equipment mentioned in this section is available from good kitchenware shops and no doubt you will spend time browsing round and building up a stock.

Icing rulers and combs

These are usually made from plastic or metal. An icing ruler has one or two straight edges and is used to smooth royal icing across the top of a cake to give a good finish. An icing comb has one or more serrated edges, which may be pulled across some icings to give a 'combed' effect. A straight-edged icing comb is used to smooth the sides of an iced cake.

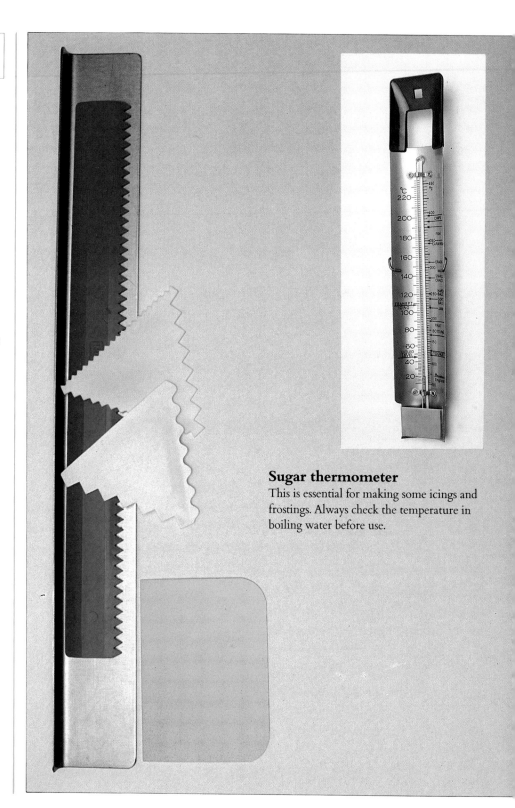

Sugar thermometer

This is essential for making some icings and frostings. Always check the temperature in boiling water before use.

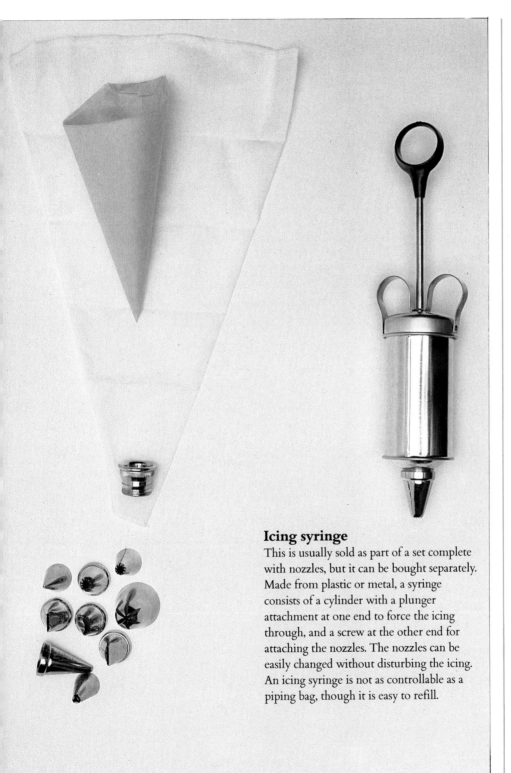

Piping bags

Nylon piping or pastry bags are available in a range of sizes. They are easy to wash and last well. If you are using two or more nozzles in the icing of a cake, paper icing bags are more convenient and are easy and cheap to make (see pages 16–17).

Icing nozzles

There are numerous nozzles available, but a basic requirement includes one or two plain writing nozzles, a selection of star nozzles and, perhaps, shell, leaf, basket and petal nozzles.

Metal nozzles are preferable to plastic ones as they give better definition. They are sold by numbers, but not all manufacturers use the same system of numbering, so always check on a chart before buying individual nozzles (see page 132 for a conversion table).

Look at the nozzles carefully before buying them. They should have no dents, the tips should be well shaped and the seams at the side should be well joined. Check that the points on a star nozzle are even. See pages 102–3 for more information on nozzles.

Icing syringe

This is usually sold as part of a set complete with nozzles, but it can be bought separately. Made from plastic or metal, a syringe consists of a cylinder with a plunger attachment at one end to force the icing through, and a screw at the other end for attaching the nozzles. The nozzles can be easily changed without disturbing the icing. An icing syringe is not as controllable as a piping bag, though it is easy to refill.

TURNTABLES AND ICING NAILS

Turntable

Though not essential, if you intend to do a lot of cake decorating, a turntable is extremely useful. The cake is placed on its board on the turntable, which revolves as required so that you can obtain a good finish to flat icing the sides.

Cake boards

These are available in a number of shapes and sizes, usually about 1cm/½in thick. They are covered in silver or gold paper and are useful to stand formal cakes on. Thin card bases are also available. Polystyrene cake bases can be obtained from some cake decorating suppliers and are excellent for practising flat or piped icing.

Icing nails and moulds

Available in a variety of different shapes, icing nails and moulds are made of plastic or metal with a metal stem. Nails are used as a rotatable base on which to ice flowers. A substitute can be made by pushing a cork on to the end of a skewer. Royal icing is piped on to lightly oiled icing moulds to make decorative shapes.

Cake markers and templates

Various rings and shapes are available in metal and plastic to help you to divide up a cake when designing a decoration. It is important that the design is even or it will look messy when finished. A pair of compasses will do equally as well.

Tweezers

Invaluable for positioning small decorations.

Paintbrush

Very useful for adding coloured details to run-outs and moulded shapes.

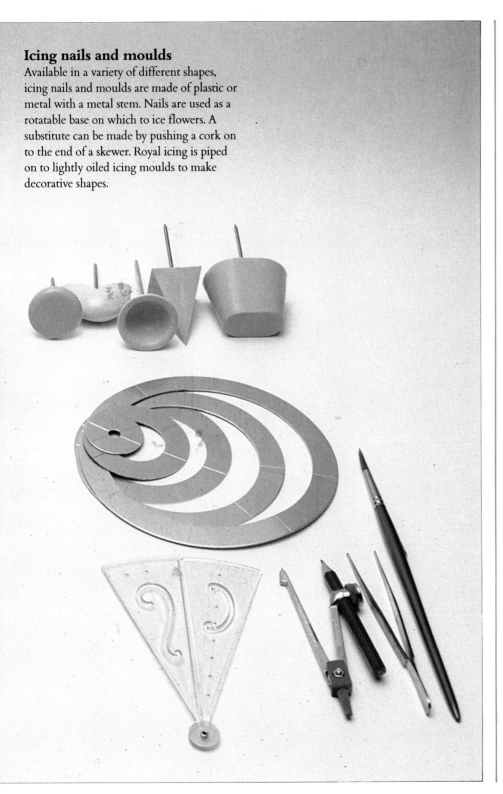

CUTTERS

There is a fantastically wide range of biscuit and aspic cutters available in all sorts of shapes, such as numbers, alphabet, animals and geometric shapes. The best definition comes from metal cutters, though some plastic ones are available. Cutters are used frequently to stamp out marzipan and rolled moulding icings, and can also be used as templates for run-out designs.

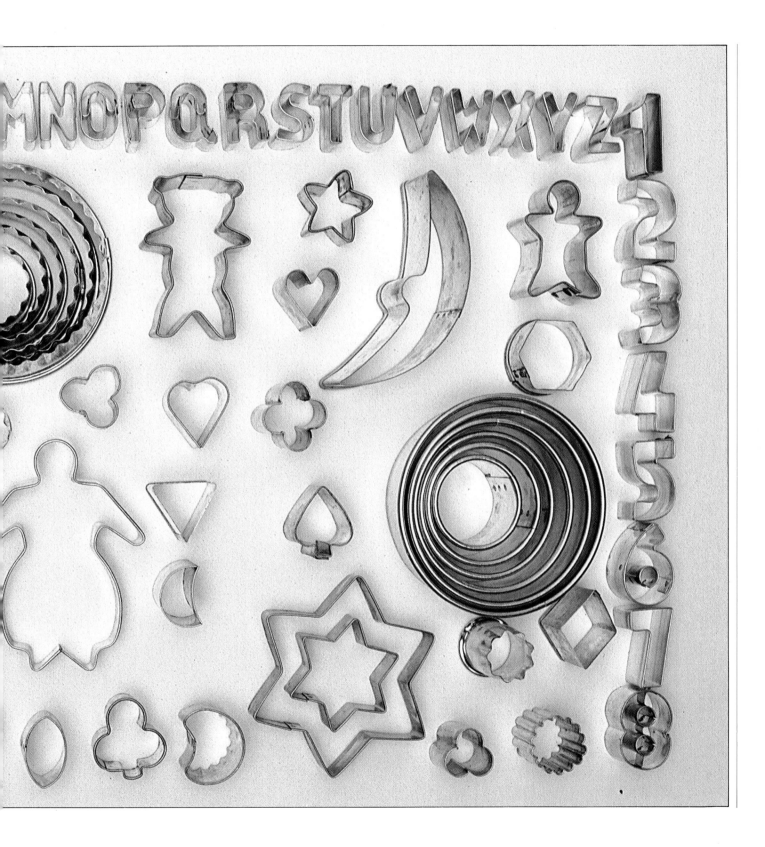

PAPER PIPING BAGS

Small paper piping bags are invaluable for piping decorations with royal, glacé or butter cream icings as they are easier to control than larger piping bags or icing syringes. They are simple to make and take any of the small icing nozzles. Make up a batch of ten at a time as you will probably use several for one cake and they can simply be discarded after use. Watch carefully all the time to see how the icing is flowing and you will quickly learn to judge the pressure and movement required to produce even, well-formed lines and shapes.

Insert a plain or writing nozzle and practise piping straight lines. Once you have mastered these, try using a star nozzle for rosettes, shells and scrolls.

To make a piping bag

1 Cut a 25cm/10in square of greaseproof or waxed paper. Fold it in half diagonally to make a triangle.

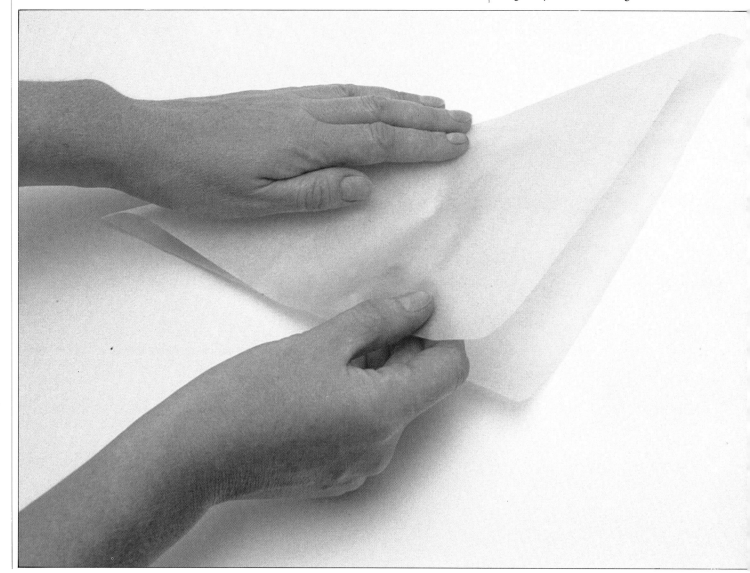

2 With the top point of the triangle facing towards you, roll in one of the side points to meet the top point.

3 Roll the other side point over the first one and bring round to the back of the top point.

4 Secure either by folding over top edges several times or by stapling them together.

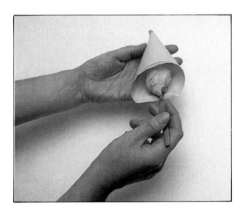

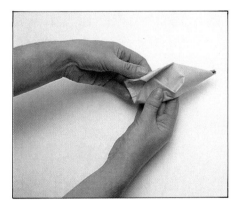

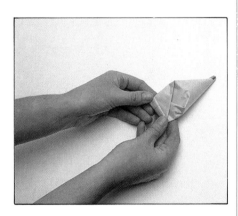

To fill a piping bag

5 Snip off the tip of the piping bag and insert the required nozzle. Spoon some icing into the base of the bag. Fill to one-half to two-thirds full. Take care not to overfill as the icing will overflow from the top or the bag will burst.

6 Fold the sides of the bag in towards the centre, then fold over the top, pushing the icing down gently towards the tip. With care the bag may be opened and refilled once or twice before being discarded.

7 You will inevitably discover the most comfortable position to hold the piping bag, but, basically, it should be held in both hands with the fingers at the sides, pressing down with the thumbs on the folded top part of the bag to squeeze out the icing. Pressing and releasing the thumbs will cause the icing to flow, then stop.

PREPARING CAKE TINS

To get the best results from decorating a cake, whether you are planning to cover it with royal icing, fondant icing or glacé icing, it is essential to work on a cake with a good smooth finish. This is why correctly lining the cake tin, to give the cake a firm, even shape, is of such vital importance. A light sponge cake will need little or no lining, while a fruit cake, particularly if it is to have a long baking time, needs proper insulation.

Lining paper

You can use either greaseproof or waxed paper to line the tin. Pack the cake well in order to get a good finish.

Whatever shape cake you use, be it round, oval, heart-shaped, square, hexagonal or octagonal, you will need only two simple techniques for shaping the paper to line curves or angles.

Cake hats

Although oven temperatures can be perfectly regulated, it may be a good idea to cut a 'hat' for the cake to prevent it from drying on top. This is a double thickness of paper approximately 5cm/2in bigger than the cake. It should rest, not on the cake batter, but on the 2.5cm/1in of paper that rises above the sides of the tin. Put it on as soon as the cake goes into the oven. This is a pointless exercise if your oven is a fan or convection model, because it will be blown off.

Lining a round tin

1 To line a round tin with greaseproof or waxed paper, place the tin base down on the greaseproof or waxed paper and draw a circle around it. Cut the circle out about 0.5cm/¼ in inside the line to allow for the thickness of the tin. Cut out another circle, the same size, for the base because you will need a double thickness for better insulation.

Lining a square tin or cake frame

1 First place the tin on the paper and mark out the base. With a cake frame, draw inside the base. With a tin, draw around it.

2 Cut out the square, remembering to make it 0.5cm/¼in smaller than your outline if you have drawn around the outside of a cake tin, to allow for the thickness of the tin. Cut another square the same size. You will need a double thickness for the base.

3 To line the sides of the tin or frame, put it on its side on the paper, Make a pencil mark where the tin touches the paper, roll the tin along until you reach the same point and make another mark. Add on 5cm/2in for overlap. Then cut a strip 5cm/2in wider than the depth of the pan, so that you have 2.5cm/1in to turn in at the base and the same amount overlapping the top.

4 To make the side lining fit the base of the tin or frame, fold it to a depth of 2.5cm/1in along its length, starting about half way along one side of the tin so that the paper joint does not end up in a corner. Use a distinguishing mark on the tin, such as a joint, or mark the tin so that you know where you started. Now turn the tin along the paper again, and mark each angle with a pencil, remembering that you are lining the inside of the tin and not the outside and allowing for the width of the tin.

2 To line the sides of the tin, put the tin on its side on the paper. Make a pencil mark where the tin touches the paper, roll the tin along until you reach the same point and make another mark. Use the joint in the tin as a starting point if there is one. Add 5cm/2in for overlap. Cut the strip 5cm/2in wider than the depth of the tin, so that you have 2.5cm/1 in to turn in at the base and the same amount overlapping the top of the tin. You need a double thickness, so cut two linings for the sides.

3 To make the side lining fit the base of the tin, fold it to a depth of 2.5cm/1in along its length. With any curved tin, snip the paper along its length, at intervals of 0.5cm/¼ in, to the depth of the fold.

4 Now slip the lining into the tin. The nicks will overlap and the paper will fit the curve of the tin snugly. When you have lined the sides of the tin with two layers of paper, drop in the two base liners. You should have a perfect fit. Brush the paper with melted butter or margarine to coat it evenly. Greaseproof paper does not need greasing.

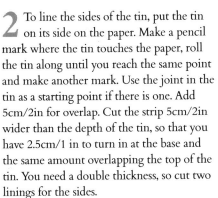

5 When you have marked all the angles of the tin, fold the paper along the pencil marks. Make a good firm crease for each angle and check that you are keeping the base parallel, so that the creases run upwards from it at a 90° angle. Now snip along the creases at 0.5cm/¼in intervals from the edge of the paper to the depth of your 2.5cm/1in fold.

6 Fold out the paper to the shape of the tin and you will see that you have very neat, right-angled corners to fit its shape. With a straight-sided tin, be it square, hexagonal or octagonal, you only have to nick the folded edges at the corners and not all the way along, as with a curved edge, to get a good fit. Slide the side lining into the tin, or into the cake frame on a baking sheet, to fit it snugly. Put in the two layers of base lining.

Lining a Swiss roll tin

1 To line a Swiss roll tin, place the tin on greaseproof or waxed paper and draw around the base. Increase the rectangle by 5cm/2in at each side to allow for the depth of the tin plus overlap. Cut out the rectangle and nick each of the corners diagonally down to the size of the original rectangle, subtracting 0.5cm/¼in for the thickness of the tin.

2 Fold the rectangle to fit the base of the tin. As you put the paper into the tin, the nicked edges will overlap to form right-angled corners. Secure the corners in position with staples or paperclips.

3 Brush the lining with melted butter or margarine and dust it with flour.

Baking sponge cakes

There is no need to line the tin if you are baking a light cake, such as a Victoria sponge cake or a Genoese or whisked sponge cake, though some people do like to put a layer of paper in the base of the pan. All you need to do is brush the tin with melted butter or margarine and then dust it with flour and sugar. Always use a brush rather than your fingers to grease the tin to ensure an even coat.

Cooling

When you turn your cake out of the tin, do not turn it on to a wire rack. The lattice pattern of the rack will be imprinted on it as the cake settles. To get a clean finish you would then have to fill in the imprints before putting on the marzipan.

Storing

Rich fruit cakes were originally made as a means of preserving summer fruit for the winter months. They would then be stored for long periods. Today, although the fruits they are made with are available all year round, there is still good reason for keeping a cake for two or three months before you decorate it. The taste of the individual ingredients becomes less distinct as the cake ages and their flavours mingle into richness.

1 To store a cake before you marzipan it, leave it in the paper you baked it in to protect it against getting knocked and having its shape spoiled.

2 The best way of keeping a cake for two or three months before marzipanning it is to wrap it first in one or two layers of greaseproof or waxed paper. Then wrap it in a tea towel or aluminium foil. Do not store it in a tin or wrap it directly in plastic wrap or aluminium foil. Unless you vacuum pack a cake inside a tin, you will be sealing stale air in with the cake. If you wrap it in plastic wrap, it will sweat. If you wrap it in foil, the natural acids in the fruit will eat through the aluminium and when you come to decorate the cake you will find the foil full of little holes.

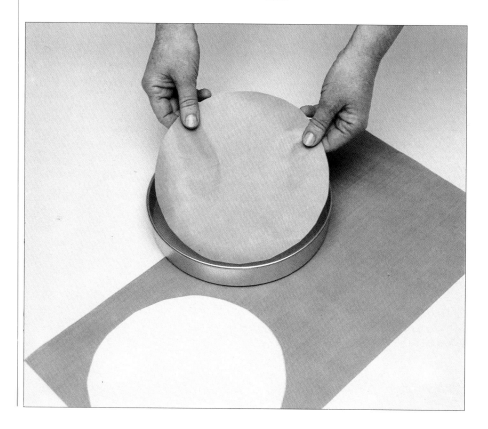

A layer of paper in the base of the tin will prevent a sponge cake from sticking.

3 While the cake is ageing, you can sprinkle it periodically with brandy or rum or any spirit of your choice. You can make holes in the cake with a skewer, then pour on a tablespoon of alcohol. Alternatively, you can buy a syringe and inject the cake to avoid it being full of large holes. Sprinkling a cake periodically definitely improves its flavour. Be careful not to add too much alcohol, however, or it will become wet and difficult to handle.

Freezing and defrosting

Sponge cakes and soft-iced cakes freeze well and can be stored over a period of months. Fruit cakes and hard-iced cakes can also be frozen, but they are better stored in a cool, dry atmosphere.

Removing a cooled cake

1 Let fruit cake cool completely in the tin. You will then find that you can lift it out of the tin quite easily by pulling the paper jutting above the sides of the tin.

2 Turn a sponge cake out on to a sheet of greaseproof or waxed paper dusted with caster sugar. The sugar will give a good finish when you turn the cake over.

3 When you peel the paper from the cooled cake it will come away cleanly, leaving the cake with perfectly smooth sides. If the paper has stuck to the cake, brush the paper with cold water and it will peel away more easily.

FREEZING

Sponge cakes

Uncooked cake batter can be stored for up to six weeks in an airtight container in the freezer. A baked sponge cake should be frozen as soon as it has cooled. Wrap it in freezer wrap and freeze it for up to four months.

Fruit cakes

A fruit cake can be frozen in the same way as a sponge cake. It is not necessary to freeze a fruit cake, however, and the freezing process actually inhibits the development of the flavour in the cake.

Soft-iced cakes

Cakes coated with a soft icing, such as buttercream or whipped cream, are particularly suitable for freezing. They must be tightly wrapped in freezer wrap, as cream-based mixtures tend to absorb flavours from foodstuffs around them if exposed to the air.

During defrosting, the cake will attract condensation and any food colours may run a little. When you take the cake from its wrappings, do not attempt to wipe away any condensation from the surface of the cake. Allow it to dry naturally.

DEFROSTING

Soft-iced cakes

The packaging should be removed before defrosting. Allow 6 to 12 hours for the cake to defrost.

Hard-iced cakes

It is essential to leave a royal or fondant iced cake in its wrapping for 24 to 48 hours, depending on its size, while it defrosts.

During defrosting, the cake will attract condensation and any food colours may run a little. When unwrapped, do not attempt to wipe away any condensation from the surface of the cake. Allow it to dry naturally.

BASIC RECIPES

CLASSIC SPONGE CAKE

The eggs are beaten over heat in this method. Use either a balloon whisk or a hand-held electric beater.

When baked, the cake should be well risen and golden in colour, and it should shrink slightly from the sides of the tin. It will feel springy to the touch. If in doubt, insert a wooden cocktail stick or skewer in the middle of the cake; it should come out clean. If any mixture adheres, leave the cake in the oven for a few minutes longer.

Lift the cake out of the oven and leave to settle in the pan for 5 minutes on a wire rack. Run a knife around the inner edge of the tin to release the cake and unclip the spring side. Invert the cake on to another wire rack, remove the tin base and peel off the paper. Leave to cool.

Ingredients

To make a 21–24cm/8½–9½in cake
4 eggs
100g/4oz/⅓ cup plus 1 tbsp caster sugar
5cm/in vanilla pod, split
100g/4oz/¾ cup plus 1 tbsp flour, sifted
180°C (350°F) mark 4 for 30–35 minutes for
a deep cake or 20 minutes for a shallow cake

1 Place the sugar and whole eggs in a large bowl set over a tin a quarter filled with simmering water, ensuring that the base of the bowl does not touch the water.

5 Sift one-third of the flour over the bowl.

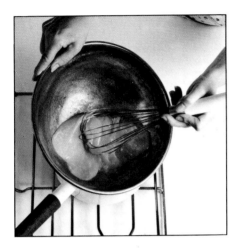

2 Lightly beat the mixture until it starts to foam and thicken.

3 Continue beating the mixture as it warms for 5-10 minutes, until it has changed to a pale colour and is rich and creamy in texture.

4 Take the bowl off the heat and continue beating until the mixture has cooled and thickened to treble its volume. A thick ribbon of batter will drop off the beater leaving a trail in the mixture for at least 5 seconds. Lightly blend in the seeds of vanilla pod.

6 Using a large metal spoon, gently fold in the flour using a figure-of-eight movement taking care not to lose any air in the mixture.

7 Sift and fold in the rest of the flour in two stages. Always move the spoon lightly and quickly, cutting down sharply through the mixture and up again, rotating the bowl as you work.

8 Scoop out the finished mixture into a lined, greased and floured spring-form tin or into two shallow sandwich tins.

WHISKED SPONGE CAKE

This classic sponge cake is made without butter and keeps fresh for quite a few days. Although you use plain flour there is no need for baking powder; what makes the cake rise so well is the increased beating, which incorporates air into the batter. Baking powder is often useful for making a cake rise, but it does have the disadvantage of drying it out. A whipped sponge cake stays moist and keeps well.

The flour and eggs should be at room temperature. Warm them slightly in a bowl over a larger bowl of warm water if your kitchen is cool. Make sure that your oven is pre-heated and your cake tins prepared before you begin. Once the batter is in the tins it should go into the oven immediately.

Ingredients

6 large eggs, room temperature
175g/6oz/¾ cup caster sugar
175g/6oz/1½ cups plain flour, sifted

Pre-heat the oven to 180°C (350°F) mark 4. Grease and flour one 20×7.5cm/8×3 in springform tin or two 20×5cm/8×2in layer pans; set aside.

1 Beat the egg yolks and sugar together until the mixture is pale and creamy and falls in a thick ribbon from the whisk. Beat the egg whites separately in a large bowl until they hold firm, creamy peaks.

2 Tip one-third of the egg snow onto the egg yolk and sugar mixture and gently fold it in using a large metal spoon.

4 Continue folding in the egg snow and flour in two further stages.

5 When all the ingredients are incorporated into the mixture it will be firm and well expanded. Pour the batter into the prepared tin(s). Bake springform about 40 minutes and layer tins 20 to 25 minutes. (See Classic Sponge, Step 4 for doneness test.) Let cake cool in the tin for a few minutes before turning on to a rack to cool completely.

 Sift one-third of the flour and, using a rubber spatula, gently fold it in.

LIGHT FRUIT CAKE

Ingredients

225g/8oz/1½ cups dried mixed fruit, chopped
¼ cup brandy, sherry
225g/8oz/1 cup unsalted butter, room temperature
240g/8oz/1 cup caster sugar
4 large eggs, room temperature
240g/8oz/2 cups plain flour, sifted

Method

1 Combine fruit and liquor or orange juice in small bowl and let soak until liquid is absorbed, at least 2 hours.

2 Preheat the oven to 170°C(350°F). Prepare an 8in springform tin by lining bottom and sides with wax paper; set aside.

3 Using an electric mixer cream the butter and sugar until light and fluffy. Lightly beat the eggs. Add a little at a time to the creamed mixture and beat well. (Do not worry if mixture appears curdled.)

4 Stir in the fruit mix. Using a rubber spatula, gently fold in the flour until completely incorporated.

5 Turn the batter into the pan, smoothing the top and then making a slight indentation in the center of the cake. Bake about 1¼ hours. Let the cake cool in the tin before turning it out onto a rack.

SWISS ROLL

You can make a Swiss roll with the whipped sponge cake batter or you can use the recipe below. Make sure that your tin is lined, greased and dusted with caster sugar, that your oven is preheated and that all your ingredients are room temperature or gently warmed before you begin.

Ingredients

100g/4oz/¾ cup plus 2 tbsp plain flour, sifted
1 tbsp cornflour
1½tsp baking powder
4 large egg whites, room temperature
a pinch of salt
200g/7oz/1 cup caster sugar
4 large egg yolks, room temperature

Method

1 Pre-heat the oven to 180°C (350°F) mark 4. Prepare a 39×26×2.5cm/15½× 10½×1in Swiss roll tin by lining it with wax paper, oiling lightly and dusting with a little caster sugar; put aside.

2 Sift the flour, cornflour (cornstarch) and baking powder together. In a large bowl beat the egg whites and salt with electric mixer until soft peaks form. Beat in 4 tablespoons caster sugar, 1 tablespoon at a time and beat until stiff peaks form.

3 In another large bowl beat the egg yolks until thick and lemon-coloured. Gradually add the water, lemon juice or orange extract and all but 1 tablespoon of the sugar and beat until the mixture falls from the beaters in an unbroken, pale yellow ribbon.

4 Gently stir about one quarter of the whites into the yolks to loosen the mixture, then fold in the remaining whites. Fold in the flour, being careful to retain as much volume as possible.

5 Pour the batter into the prepared tin, spreading it evenly. Tap the tin lightly on the counter to remove any air bubbles. Bake 12 to 15 minutes, until cake tests done.

6 Sprinkle a sheet of wax or greaseproof paper liberally with caster sugar. To help prevent the cake from breaking or cracking when removing it from the tin, it is a good idea to lay the paper on top of a dish cloth that has been wrung out in hot water.

7 When the cake is done, turn the pan upside down onto the sugar sprinkled paper. Remove the lining paper as quickly as possible — if it sticks, dampen it slightly. Cut off any crisp cake edges with a sharp knife. Spread the cake fairly generously with warmed jam. Starting from short side, roll cake tightly for the first turn and then more loosely.

8 If you want to fill the Swiss roll with whipped cream or buttercream, roll it up with the paper inside and let it stand until completely cold. Unroll the cake gently; remove and discard the paper. Spread the cake with filling and roll it back up again. (You often get a better-looking cake if you use jam only since just one rolling is necessary.)

MADEIRA CAKE

Madeira cake can be used for all the cakes which involve a lot of cutting and shaping before the marzipan and icing are added. In order to achieve good angles and curves the cake should be compact in texture and able to withstand pressure while remaining moist and flavourful.

Ingredients

175g/6oz/¾ cup unsalted butter, room temperature
175g/6oz/¾ cup caster sugar
3 large eggs, room temperature
175g/6oz/1½ cups self-raising flour, sifted
50g/2oz/½ cup plain flour, sifted
1tbsp lemon juice
2tsp lemon zest
1tsp vanilla

Method

1 Pre-heat the oven to 180°C (350°F) Mark 4. Pre-heat a 20cm/8in springform or 20cm/8in square tin; set aside.

2 Using an electric mixer cream the butter and the sugar until mixture is light and fluffy. Add the eggs one at a time, followed by a spoonful of the self-raising flour, and beat thoroughly.

3 Sift the remaining flours together. Fold gently into the batter using a rubber spatula. Try to retain as much volume as possible. Fold in the lemon juice, lemon zest and vanilla.

4 Turn the mixture into the prepared tin(s), smoothing the top. Bake about 45 to 50 minutes, until cake shrinks slightly from sides of pan. Let the cake cool in the pan for 5 to 10 minutes. Sprinkle wax or greaseproof paper liberally with sugar. Turn the cake out on to the paper, remove the lining paper and let cake cool completely.

USEFUL FILLINGS

APRICOT GLAZE

This is frequently spread over a sponge or sandwich cake before the layer of icing is applied. The sticky glaze ensures there are no loose crumbs that could stick to the icing and spoil the finished effect. It is also used to attach decorations to a cake, such as desiccated coconut or chopped nuts, to attach marzipan to a rich fruit cake, and as a glaze for fresh fruits on a gateau.

Ingredients

225g/8oz/¾ cup apricot jam
2tbsp water
squeeze of lemon juice

Method

1 Place the jam, water and lemon juice in a small saucepan. Heat gently until the jam has dissolved, then boil for 1 minute. Strain and cool.

2 Any spare glaze can be stored in the refrigerator in a screw-top jar for several weeks. Warm the glaze gently to re-use.

Variation

REDCURRANT GLAZE. Replace the apricot jam with redcurrant jelly. Omit water. No need to strain.

PRALINE

A delicious mixture of whole, unblanched almonds toasted with sugar to form a caramel. The caramel is usually finely chopped or ground and may be used as a decoration, or to flavour butter creams or fresh whipped cream.

Ingredients

100g/4oz/¾ cup unblanched whole almonds
100g/4oz/½ cup caster sugar

Method

1 Place the almonds and sugar in a saucepan over a very low heat. Stir continually until the nuts are toasted and the sugar has caramelized to a rich, golden colour.

2 Lightly butter or oil a baking sheet and pour the praline over the sheet. Leave until completely cold, then break into pieces.

3 Finely chop or grind the praline, or place in a thick plastic bag and pound it with a rolling pin. The praline may then be sieved if wished. Store in an airtight container.

STOCK SYRUP

This is simply sugar dissolved in water, which can be flavoured with liqueur or spirit, and is used to moisten sponge layers before assembling them with fresh cream or icing. It is also used to soften fondant icing so that it can be poured over a cake. Stock syrup may be stored in the refrigerator for several weeks in a screw-top jar or other container.

Ingredients

100g/4oz/½ cup granulated sugar
150ml/¼pt/⅔ cup water

Method

1 Place the sugar and water in a saucepan and dissolve gently. Bring to the boil and boil for 1 minute. Flavour with any liqueur or spirit to the desired strength.

CARAMEL

Sugar syrup can be boiled until it reaches a golden caramel colour. Once this has set hard it can be broken into tiny pieces and used very effectively as a decoration. With a gas hob it is possible to put only sugar into a pan and heat it gently until caramelized. But with an electric hob, it is better to make a strong sugar syrup first and then boil it to a caramel stage.

Apricot glaze

Redcurrant glaze

Ingredients

100g/4oz/½ cup caster or granulated sugar
3tbsp water

Method

1 Dissolve the sugar in the water in a saucepan over gentle heat. Bring to the boil and boil to a golden caramel.

2 Pour onto a buttered or oiled baking sheet and leave until set hard. Break into tiny pieces. This does not store well, so make only sufficient for the decoration.

3 Caramel may also be used as a coating, rather like an icing. In this case, pour it directly onto the sponge layer and leave until starting to set. Mark out the portions of the cake with an oiled knife, otherwise the cake will be impossible to cut when the caramel is hard.

Stock syrup

Caramel

Praline

CREAM PATISSIERE

Ingredients

2 egg yolks
3tbsp plain flour
1½tbsp cornflour
50g/2oz/¼ cup caster sugar
275ml/10fl oz/1¼ cups milk
1 egg white
3 or 4 drops vanilla extract

This quantity is sufficient for filling and topping a 20cm/8-in sponge cake.

Method

1 Lightly beat yolks in a small bowl. Add the sugar gradually and cream well. Sift flour and cornflour together. Beat into mixture along with half of the milk.

2 Bring the remaining milk to the boil. Slowly stir it into the egg mixture and blend well. Return mixture to the milk pan and stir over medium heat until the mixture reaches boiling point. Set aside.

3 Beat the egg white until stiff. Take about a quarter of the blended cream from the pan and fold the beaten egg white gently into it. Then return the mixture to the pan and cook over a gentle heat for 3 to 4 minutes, folding the mixture occasionally and adding the vanilla. Turn it into a bowl to cool.

Confectioner's custard and whipped cream RIGHT make lavish fillings and toppings. The cake is filled and decorated with piped whipped cream, candied fruit, almonds and chocolate sprinkes.

GINGER CREAM FILLING

Ingredients

275g/10oz/1¼ cups confectioner's custard
50g/2oz/⅓ cup dried ginger
grated lemon zest, finely sliced
2-3tsp ginger syrup
2tbsp whipped cream

Method

1 Combine the custard, ginger and lemon zest in a bowl. Stir in the ginger syrup and fold in the cream.

2 If the filling is too thin, add some cake crumbs. Pineapple may be substituted for ginger.

CONFECTIONER'S CUSTARD

Ingredients

275ml/10fl oz/1¼ cups milk
2tbsp cornflour
2 egg yolks
2tbsp caster sugar
½tsp vanilla extract

Method

1 In a small saucepan warm the milk gently. Blend in the cornflour. Bring to the boil, stirring, and simmer for 5 minutes. Remove from the heat and let cool.

2 Stir in the egg yolks and flavouring. Do not be tempted to add the yolks before the custard has cooled, as they will curdle and start to cook.

3 Stir in the sugar, return to the heat and cook gently for a few minutes, without allowing it to boil. Once the sugar has dissolved, cover the pan and let cool.

WHAT CAN GO WRONG

Knowing how to test a cake correctly is a simple but invaluable skill.

Because a cake bakes from the outside in, it is the centre of the cake that you need to test to see if it is done. If you cut a cake and find that the inside is paler, this means that it is not baked properly. You should be able to tell if a cake is baked by gently pressing it with your finger. If the cake springs back, it is done.

A simple, but infallible test for a fruit cake is the skewer test. Insert a skewer in the centre of the cake and leave it there for 5 seconds. If it comes out clean, the cake is cooked. If you do not leave the skewer for 5 seconds, it will come out clean whether the cake is cooked or not.

You can also test a sponge cake to see if it is done with a skewer. Stick the skewer into the centre of the cake, and if it comes out clean, the cake is done. But take care, because sticking a skewer into a sponge cake or Genoese cake can make it collapse.

Sponge cake

This sponge cake was turned out on to a wire rack. The cake is imprinted with the pattern of the rack, and some of it has stuck and pulled away from the cake.

The cake has not risen because the oven was too hot — the leavening agent was cooked before it could work.

Unrisen sponge

This sponge cake has not risen well. There is too much egg in it and the ingredients were too cold to start with.

Chapter Two:
SIMPLE ICING RECIPES AND TECHNIQUES

This section demonstrates the classic decoration of sponge cakes with soft fillings and coatings, including very easy designs with a dusting of confectioner's sugar and more elaborate piped buttercream coverings.

The techniques are simple but create attractive effects, and include diamond marking, cobweb icing and feather icing, grooving, swirling and peaking; two ways to decorate a Swiss roll, and coating sponge cake with soft fondant icing. All the cakes are ideal for everyday or even to celebrate an informal festive occasion. Following these demonstrations will give you practice in using some of the basic tools of the trade — the turntable, metal spatulas, cake combs, pastry bags and food colour — and at the same time help you develop your skills.

QUICK AND EASY DECORATIVE TOPPINGS

Apart from icings, there are many simple yet highly effective ways of decorating a cake, using whipped cream, meringue or dredged icing sugar.

Decorating with fresh cream

Fresh cream makes a very good filling and 'icing' for a whisked sponge cake, transforming it into something quite special.

Double cream is the best cream to use as it whips well and holds its shape when piped. Whipping cream has a lower fat content and is less firm than double cream. It can be used far spreading, but is not as good for piping. There are commercial cream substitutes in powder form, which pipe very well when reconstituted with milk.

Both cream and cream substitutes are piped through a large star nozzle rather than the smaller icing nozzles.

Whipped cream may be used as the finished covering of a cake. For the sides it can be smoothed or serrated using an icing comb, or used as a base for another covering, such as chopped nuts or langues de chats biscuits. The addition of fresh fruit on the top of the cake adds colour and texture. The fruit can be arranged on the surface and glazed with apricot or redcurrant glaze (page 28) then piped with whirls of whipped cream, or the cream can be the main decoration with a little fruit for added colour.

To whip fresh cream

Place the cream in a bowl and, using a hand-held electric mixer or a balloon whisk, whisk the cream until it forms soft peaks. Be careful not to overwhip the cream as it will become very thick and granules will appear. This texture cannot be remedied.

Decorating with icing sugar

Dredged icing sugar is the easiest decorative topping. Spoon a little icing sugar into a sieve and sprinkle it over the surface of the cake. Use a palette knife to lightly score the surface with diagonal lines to create a simple pattern.

More elaborate results can be achieved by sprinking the icing sugar over a doily, then carefully removing it.

Cocoa powder or drinking chocolate powder can be used as a second sprinkling to give a more intricate design.

DECORATING WITH MERINGUE

Meringue mixture pipes very well and effectively, and can be used in a similar way to fresh cream as a decoration. It should be browned very quickly for 2-3 minutes in a pre-heated oven set at the hottest setting. Any other decoration, such as whipped cream or fresh fruit, should be added afterwards.

Ingredients

2 egg whites
pinch salt
½ cup/100g/4oz caster sugar

1 Whisk the egg whites with the salt until stiff.

2 Add the sugar a spoonful at a time, whisking thoroughly between each addition until a thick white meringue mixture is formed. Use at once.

3 Spread the sides of the cake with a thin layer of meringue. A thicker layer can be used as insulation for an ice-cream filling.

4 Spread the top of the cake with an even layer. Place the remaining mixture in a nylon piping bag fitted with a large star nozzle and pipe a decorative pattern.

5 Place the cake in a pre-heated oven for 2-3 minutes until golden. Add any further decorations.

6 A meringue-covered cake is best eaten straightaway, but if it has an ice-cream filling, it can be kept in the freezer for an hour or two until ready to serve.

Decorating with nuts and coconut

Nuts and coconut are widely used in simple cake decoration, particularly in combination with butter-cream, whipped cream and glacé icing. Their flavour and texture contrast well with sweet, soft toppings and fillings. They also make very attractive decorations. Illustrated here are a variety of ground and whole nuts, blanched and unblanched almonds, and plain and coloured coconut.

GLACÉ ICING

This very simple icing is used to decorate sandwich or sponge cakes, but it is also useful when decorating pastries and biscuits or cookies. It may be coloured with edible food colourings and flavoured in many ways. If adding a liquid flavouring, such as a liqueur, omit an equivalent amount of the water. The quantity given in the basic recipe will cover the top and sides of a 20cm/8in cake; use half the quantity for the top only.

Ingredients

225g/8oz/2 cups icing sugar, sifted
2tbsp warm water

1 Sift the sugar into a bowl and add the warm water. Beat well until smooth and thick enough to coat the back of a wooden spoon. Add a little extra liquid if necessary. If you add too much liquid, simply sift in more sugar to achieve the required consistency. Use at once.

To coat the top of a cake

Place the cake on a plate or board. If desired, brush the top with a thin layer of apricot glaze (page 28).

Pour or spoon the icing on to the centre of the cake. Using a palette knife, spread the icing carefully to the edges. Dip the clean palette knife in hot water and smooth the icing.

Tap the plate gently on the work surface to release any air bubbles and give a smooth finish. Any small air bubbles may be burst with a pin. Leave to set for at least 1 hour.

An alternative method of coating the top of a cake is to make a greaseproof or waxed paper collar about 1cm/½in deeper than the cake. Wrap the collar tightly round the cake and secure with a paper clip. Pour the icing on to the cake and spread to the edges. Leave icing to set before carefully removing the collar.

If decorations are to be added, press these into the icing before it sets completely. If further piped icing is desired, pipe this when the base coat is completely set.

To coat the top and sides of a cake

Follow the basic rules for coating the top, but allow the icing to flow down the sides and carefully smooth it with a wetted palette knife. Once the icing is set, the excess may be scraped from the plate or board. An alternative method is to place the cake on a wire rack over a plate or piece of greaseproof or waxed paper, and allow the excess icing to drip through. Once the icing is set, the cake can be carefully removed from the rack.

Using glacé icing

Apart from its use as a coating, glacé icing may be piped, using a plain or writing nozzle (no. 2 or no. 3). However, it is not firm enough to make rosettes and whirls. Piped rosettes or swirls of butter cream may be added to an iced cake for further decoration.

Variations

Liquid flavourings must be used in place of water and *not* in addition.

VANILLA. Use 1 tsp vanilla essence in place of the same amount of water.

ORANGE, LEMON, LIME, GRAPEFRUIT OR OTHER FRUIT JUICE. Substitute strained fruit juice for the measured amount of water.

COFFEE. Dissolve 1 tbsp instant coffee powder in the measured water.

CHOCOLATE. Substitute 2 tbsp sifted cocoa powder for an equal quantity of icing sugar.

LIQUEUR. Substitute liqueur for an equal amount of water. Use at least 1 tbsp liqueur, but increase this if wished.

COLOURED. Add a few drops of the appropriate edible food colouring.

BUTTER CREAMS

These are perhaps the most versatile icings for sponge and sandwich cakes as they can be used for filling and topping a cake, as well as covering the sides as a base for decoration. They pipe well and are easily flavoured and coloured. Butter gives a better flavour, but margarine may be used if wished. The basic recipe will fill and cover the top of a 20cm/8in sandwich cake, or cover top and sides.

Ingredients

100g/4oz/½ cup butter, at room temperature
225g/8oz/2 cups confectioners' icing sugar, sifted
1-2tbsp milk or 1 large egg yolk (optional)

Method

1 Beat the butter until light and fluffy, then beat in the icing sugar a little at a time until well mixed. If wished, beat in the milk or egg yolk to give a richer icing.

2 If not required immediately, store in an airtight container in the refrigerator. Leave in a warm place to soften slightly before use.

CREME AU BEURRE

A deliciously rich, smooth butter cream. Always use unsalted butter as salted butter gives too strong a flavour. This quantity will fill and top a 20cm/8in sandwich cake plus extra for piped decorations.

Ingredients

75g/3oz/½ cup and 1tbsp granulated sugar
4tbsp water
2 egg yolks
175g/6oz/¾ cup unsalted butter

1 Place the sugar in a saucepan with the water and heat gently until dissolved. Bring to the boil and boil until the temperature reaches 108°C/226°F on a sugar thermometer.

2 Beat the egg yolks in a bowl until pale. Pour the syrup in a thin stream on to the egg yolks, whisking all the time. Continue to whisk until the mixture is thick and cold.

3 Beat the butter until light and fluffy. Gradually beat the egg mixture into the butter until evenly blended. Use at once to fill and decorate.

Variations for butter cream and crème au beurre

VANILLA. Add 1–2tsp vanilla essence to taste.

PEPPERMINT. Add 1–2tsp peppermint essence to taste and colour with green edible food colouring.

LEMON, ORANGE, LIME OR GRAPEFRUIT. Add 1–2tbsp strained fruit juice, and grated rind if wished. Colouring may also be added.

CHOCOLATE. Add up to 100g/4oz/4 squares melted and cooled chocolate, or 4tbsp sifted cocoa powder.

COFFEE. Add 1–2tbsp instant coffee powder dissolved in 1–2tbsp hot water, or use coffee essence.

FRUIT PURÉE. Add up to generous 100ml/4fl/½ cup very thick fruit purée, such as strawberry, raspberry, apricot or blackcurrant.

LIQUEUR. Add up to 2tbsp of the chosen liqueur.

MARSHMALLOW BUTTER CREAM

A light and fluffy icing made by beating softened butter into a meringue mixture. The meringue may be made either by whisking egg whites and icing sugar over simmering water until stiff, or by boiling a sugar syrup to the hard ball stage and adding that to stiffly whisked egg whites. Both versions can be flavoured in the same way as butter cream and crème au beurre. Recipe 1 is sufficient to fill and top a 20cm/8in sandwich cake. Recipe 2 is sufficient to fill and cover a 20-23cm/8-9in cake.

FONDANT BUTTER CREAM

This is a good way of using up leftover fondant icing (see page 62). It has a creamy texture similar to crème au beurre. The quantity given is sufficient to fill and cover a 20cm/8in cake.

Ingredients

175g/6oz/¾ cup fondant (page 62)
1-2tbsp stock syrup (page 28)
175g/6oz/¾ cup butter, softened

Method

1 Warm the fondant with the syrup, in a bowl over hot water, until it is soft enough to beat.

2 Beat the butter until fluffy, then beat in the cooled fondant. Flavour as desired (see right) and use at once.

Ingredients (Recipe 1)

2 egg whites
125g/4oz/1cup confectioners' icing sugar, sifted
150g/5oz/½ cup + 2tbsp butter, softened

1 Place the egg whites and sugar in a bowl over a pan of simmering water. Whisk for 5-7 minutes until the mixture is thick and white. Remove from the heat and continue whisking until cool.

2 Beat the butter until fluffy, then fold in the meringue mixture. Flavour as desired and use at once.

Ingredients (Recipe 2)

225g/8oz/1 cup granulated sugar
100ml/4fl oz/½ cup water
4 egg whites
225g/8oz/1 cup butter, softened

1 Place the sugar and water in a saucepan and heat gently until dissolved. Bring to the boil, and boil until the syrup reaches the hard ball stage on a sugar thermometer: 121°C/250°F.

2 Meanwhile, whisk the egg whites until stiff. As soon as the syrup is ready, pour it in a thin stream on to the egg whites, whisking all the time. Continue to whisk until the mixture stands in stiff peaks. Leave to cool.

3 Beat the butter until fluffy, then fold in the meringue mixture. Flavour as desired and use at once.

Variations

Recipe 1

LEMON AND ORANGE. Add grated rind ½ lemon or orange and 1tbsp juice.

CHOCOLATE. Add 50g/2oz/2squares melted chocolate, cooled.

COFFEE. Add 2-3tsp coffee essence or instant coffee powder dissolved in a little hot water.

Recipe 2

Use up to double the amount of the above flavourings.

To decorate the sides of a cake

The sides of a cake may be spread with a butter cream, then left smooth, swirled with a knife or combed with an icing comb. If, however, a further coating, such as chopped nuts, is required the cake may first be spread with either apricot glaze or butter cream. For gâteaux, crème au beurre or fresh cream is usually used.

Spread the sides of the cake with a thin layer of butter cream or brush with apricot glaze.

Spread the chosen coating on a sheet of greaseproof or waxed paper and, holding the cake between the palms of your hands, gently roll it over the coating until evenly covered.

Sometimes a cake may be too delicate for this, in which case, the coating ingredient must be pressed against the sides of the cake using a palette knife.

Suitable coatings include: chopped nuts; toasted coconut; chocolate vermicelli; grated or chopped chocolate.

Simple ways to use butter cream

Butter cream is a smooth spreadable icing, which can be easily made into an effective pattern.

Spread an even layer over the cake then:

1 Use a fork to make a circular design on a round cake, or straight or wavy lines on a square cake. If wished, mark the cake into section with a knife.

2 Using a palette knife, work the icing from side to side, slightly overlapping the lines made by the knife each time.

3 Using a palette knife, start from the centre of the cake and make swirls to the edge, each time overlapping the previous swirl.

4 Use a palette knife to make a general swirling pattern.

Butter cream also pipes very well and can be used in many ways to give a decorative effect. For more information on piping techniques, see pages 110–21.

Using a star nozzle, pipe one of the following designs:

1 Straight parallel lines in one or more contrasting colours.

2 Rosettes in lines or circles, in one or more contrasting colours.

3 Large shells or rosettes around the edge of the cake.

4 A lattice effect over the surface of the cake.

5 Scrolls on each marked portion of the cake.

6 Pipe elongated loops from the centre to the outside edge of the cake and fill each loop with jam.

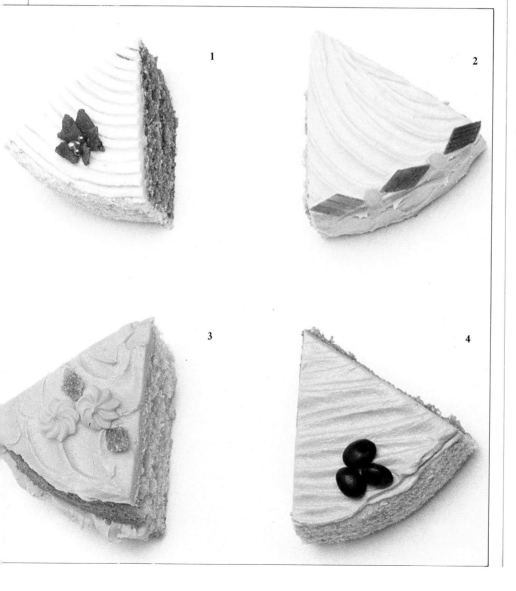

1

2

3

4

FUDGE ICINGS

These icings are very soft and can be swirled easily to give a decorative effect. Once cold, they set firm on the surface, yet remain soft underneath.

The basic recipe is a smooth fudge icing that turns golden during cooking, so don't worry and think you've spoiled it! It is sufficient to cover an 18-20cm/7-8in ring cake or a 20cm/8in sandwich cake.

Ingredients

150ml/¼pt/generous ½ cup single or soured cream
225g/8oz/1 cup + 2tbsp caster sugar
100g/4oz/½ cup unsalted butter

Method

1 Place the cream and sugar in a saucepan and heat very gently until dissolved.

2 Increase the heat and boil the mixture for about 15 minutes until it reaches the soft ball stage on a sugar thermometer: 116°C/240°F. Stir frequently to prevent the mixture sticking to the pan. If you don't have a sugar thermometer, a small spoonful of the mixture should form a soft ball when dropped into cold water.

3 Leave to cool for about 2 minutes, then beat in the butter, a little at a time. If the icing starts to look oily, add an ice cube and beat vigorously until it has melted; this will return the icing to a good consistency.

4 Coat the cake immediately, allowing the icing to run down the sides and using a palette knife as little as possible, or allow to thicken and spread over the cake.

Variations

CHOCOLATE. Beat 50g/2oz/2squares plain chocolate, broken in pieces, with the butter.
NUT. Beat in 25-50g/1-2oz/¼-½ cup finely chopped toasted nuts.
COFFEE. Beat in 1tbsp instant coffee powder dissolved in 1tsp hot water.

LEMON FUDGE ICING

Ingredients

Sufficient to cover an 18cm/7in cake
40g/1½oz/3tbsp butter
2tbsp lemon juice
225g/8oz/1⅔ cup confectioners'
icing sugar, sifted
grated rind ½ lemon

Method

1 Melt the butter and the lemon juice in a saucepan over a gentle heat. Bring to the boil. Remove from the heat, add the sugar and lemon rind and beat well. Allow to cool slightly, then use at once.

Variations

CARAMEL. Substitute milk and brown sugar for the lemon juice and icing sugar. Omit lemon rind.

COFFEE. Substitute milk for the lemon juice; add 1tbsp instant coffee powder. Omit lemon rind.

CHOCOLATE. Substitute milk for the lemon juice; add 1–2tbsp cocoa powder. Omit lemon rind.

ORANGE OR LIME. Substitute orange or lime juice and rind for the lemon juice and rind.

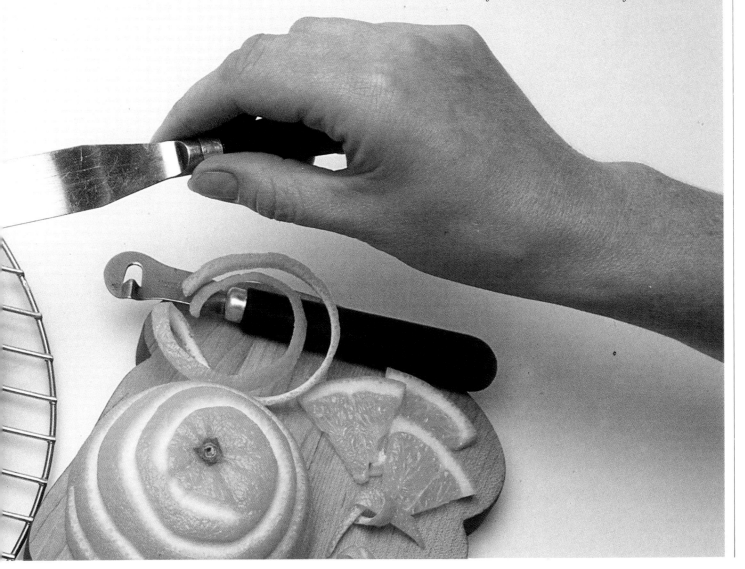

FROSTINGS

These have the texture of marshamallow and they spread and swirl easily. They set quickly so have your utensils and cake decorations ready before you start.

AMERICAN FROSTING

This frosting is easily flavoured and coloured. In order to make it successfully, however, it is best to use a sugar thermometer. The quantity given is sufficient to cover the top and sides of a 23cm/9in sandwich cake. Half quantity is sufficient to cover a 23cm/9in ring cake.

Ingredients

350g/12oz/1½ cups granulated sugar
150ml/¼pt/⅔ cup water
2 egg whites
pinch salt or cream of tartar

1 Place the sugar and water in a saucepan and heat gently until dissolved.

2 Bring to the boil and boil steadily, without stirring, for about 10–15 minutes until a sugar thermometer registers the soft ball stage: 116°C/240°F. Remove the sugar syrup from the heat.

3 Whisk the egg whites with the salt until stiff. Slowly pour the sugar syrup on to the egg whites, whisking all the time until cool and thick.

4 As this takes 5–10 minutes, it is best to use a hand-held electric mixer. Add any chosen flavourings and colourings, and use at once.

Spreading and swirling a frosting is a simple and effective way to cover a cake.

SEVEN-MINUTE FROSTING

This gets its name from the fact that it takes seven minutes to make! It is similar in texture to American frosting, but can be made without a sugar thermometer. Sufficient to cover an 18–20cm/7–8in cake.

Ingredients

1 egg white
175g/6oz/¾ cup caster sugar or soft brown sugar
2tbsp hot water
pinch salt or cream of tartar

Method

1 Put all the ingredients in a bowl over a saucepan of hot water.

2 Whisk until the mixture thickens sufficiently to stand in soft peaks; this should take about 7 minutes using a hand-held electric mixer. Use at once.

Variations

LEMON OR OTHER CITRUS FRUITS. Beat in grated rind of a medium lemon with 1tbsp juice. Add a few drops of edible food colouring if desired.
COFFEE. Whisk in 2tbsp instant coffee powder dissolved in 2tsp hot water.
CHOCOLATE. Whisk in 4tbsp cocoa powder dissolved in 2tbsp hot water.

JAM FROSTING

This is a very much reduced sugar icing for those who are more calorie conscious! Do not make this too far in advance of using and eating, as it is not as stable as those frostings with a lot of added sugar. Sufficient to cover a 20cm/8in cake.

Ingredients

3 egg whites
pinch salt
4tbsp jam, warmed and sieved

1 Whisk the egg whites and salt until stiff enough to stand in peaks.

2 Whisk in the jam and continue to whisk for a further minute.

VANILLA, PEPPERMINT OR ALMOND. Whisk in 2–3tsp of the appropriate essence. Add a few drops of green food colouring with the peppermint essence, if wished.
CARAMEL. Substitute soft brown sugar for the granulated sugar.

CHOCOLATE ICINGS

There are many different chocolate icings to make, but the easiest one is simply melted chocolate, though this does set hard and is rather difficult to cut unless you use a hot knife.

Very simple, but still very rich icings can be made by just adding a little butter or fresh cream to melted chocolate. This softens the chocolate, making it more manageable and sometimes suitable for piping. Spirit, particularly rum, is often added.

Butter cream and crème au beurre may be flavoured with melted chocolate, and glacé icing can be made with some sifted cocoa powder in addition to the icing sugar.

What kind of chocolate to use

There are many types of chocolate available and it may be confusing when it comes to deciding which one you should use for what purpose. Basically, chocolate can be divided into three categories.

1 Chocolate cake covering. This is usually found in the baking section of the supermarket. It is not a true chocolate bar, but melts and spreads easily and is perfectly acceptable for everyday and children's cakes. It is also slightly softer in texture than a true chocolate bar and is, therefore, easier to grate or to make into chocolate curls.

2 Cooking chocolate. This is available in bars and as drops. It is very good for all icings and chocolate cookery.

3 Superior dessert chocolate. An expensive choice, which should be used only for very special icings.

GANACHE

This is one of the richest chocolate icings imaginable! It is made from chocolate and double cream, which are melted together, then mixed to a dark, smooth icing. It can be spread as it is, or whipped to lighten it and increase the volume. Liqueur or spirit may be added as desired. Once whipped, ganache pipes extremely well. The quantity given is sufficient to fill and cover a 20cm/8in cake.

Ingredients

250ml/8fl oz/1 cup double cream
225g/8oz/8 squares plain chocolate

1 Heat the cream to just below boiling. Remove from the heat.

2 Break the chocolate into small pieces and add to the cream. Leave for several minutes until the chocolate has melted. Beat well, then leave to cool.

3 If wished, whip the cooled chocolate icing until pale and doubled in bulk. Add spirit as desired. Use at once.

MOCHA ICING

This is a very dark chocolate icing, flavoured with coffee. Pour over a cake and allow it to flow down the sides. Use a palette knife as little as possible to spread it and it will set to a glorious shine. The quantity given is sufficient to cover a 20–23cm/8–9in cake.

Ingredients

100g/4oz/$\frac{1}{2}$ cup caster sugar
3tbsp cocoa powder
2tbsp water
1tsp instant coffee powder
75g/3oz/6tbsp butter

1 Heat the sugar, cocoa, water and coffee in a saucepan over a gentle heat, stirring all the time with a wooden spoon, until the sugar has dissolved. Bring to the boil and simmer for 1 minute. Remove from the heat.

2 Beat in the butter and allow to cool sufficiently to coat the back of a wooden spoon. Use at once.

Mocha icing

Chocolate frosting

THICK CHOCOLATE ICING

Ingredients

To make a 21–24cm/8½–9½in cake
100g/3½oz plain chocolate
½tbsp unsalted butter
165ml/5½fl oz/⅔ cup water

Method

1 Melt the chocolate and butter together with 1tbsp of boiling water in a heat-proof bowl set over simmering water. Draw off the heat and stir to blend.

2 Put the water in a heavy-based pan, add the sugar and boil to the thread stage (102°C/215°F; 20 seconds).

3 Stir the chocolate liquid straight into the syrup and replaced the pan on the heat. Boil gently for 5 minutes when the icing will have thickened. Test a few drops on a plate — it should feel sticky.

4 Pour the icing straight over the apricot-glazed cake, tipping the wire rack back and forth so that the icing runs all over the top. Do not use a spatula on the surface, but smooth more on the sides.

5 Decorate with fruits and nuts immediately, although piped decoration should be applied when the chocolate icing has cooled completely. The icing will set with a high gloss but will dull a little after 24 hours. The cake may then be stored in the refrigerator without spoiling.

CHOCOLATE FROSTING

This is a spreadable icing that can be swirled to give a decorative, yet quick finish to a cake. The quantity given is sufficient to cover a 20cm/8in cake.

Ingredients

100g/4oz/4 squares plain or milk chocolate
25g/1oz/2tbsp butter
5tbsp milk
300g/10oz/2–2¼ cups icing sugar

Method

Melt the chocolate and butter in the milk in a saucepan over a gentle heat. Add the icing sugar and beat well. Allow to cool.

SOFT CHOCOLATE ICING

Ingredients

100g/3½oz plain chocolate
75g/3oz/¾ cup caster sugar, sifted
3tbsp unsalted butter, cut in pieces
2tbsp water

1 Melt the chocolate in a bowl set over simmering water.

2 Stir in the sugar and the butter and continue stirring until the butter has melted and the mixture is smooth.

3 Remove from the heat and add the water, 1tbsp at a time. Use while lukewarm. Do not touch!

DECORATIVE TECHNIQUES

Triangular top

1 Spread one layer of a Victoria sponge cake with butter cream and pipe two rows of shells around the edge. Cut the second cake in half horizontally and use the bottom piece for other purposes. Dredge the top with icing sugar, making a pattern through a doily. Cut it carefully into three. Position the pieces on top of the cake with a cake slice.

2 Pipe lines of cream shells over the joints. Decorate the top with split almonds, angelica and a cherry in the centre.

Peaking

1 Cover the top of the cake with butter icing and use a metal spatula to pull it up into peaks.

2 Sprinkle the top with coloured sprinkles and add a gold ribbon for a festive effect.

Split top decoration

1 Spread one layer of a Victoria sponge cake with butter cream. Draw a line over the cream with a skewer to give the halfway mark. Pipe a double row of butter cream shells around half the cake edge, piping them more heavily on the centre edges than at the sides. Do the same around the other half if you want to create a butterfly effect with the finished cake.

2 Use a very sharp serrated knife and carefully slice the second cake in half horizontally. Dredge the top with icing sugar and cut the cake in half. Mark a decorative pattern in the icing sugar with a skewer as shown.

The chocolate cake is diamond marked with a border of piped shells.

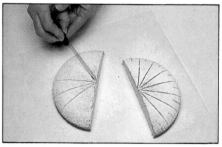

Diamond marking

1 Cover the sides of the cake with chocolate sprinkles and spread the top with chocolate butter cream. Make a diamond pattern by pulling a skewer through the butter cream as shown.

2 Pipe simple shells round the edge of the top of the cake using star tip No. 11 or 12 and chocolate butter cream.

3 Being careful not to touch the top of the cake with your fingers, which would leave prints, place the two halves in position on top of the butter cream shells using a cake slice. One half should stand open resting on the butter cream shells or both if you have piped shells around both sides.

4 Pipe a line of butter cream shells across the joint and decorate with cherries and angelica.

2 Finish decorating the cake with green candied cherries, cut into segments and positioned on the sides between the rosettes. Make a flower shape of candied pineapple with a yellow candied cherry for its centre on the top.

Rosettes

1 To make rosettes, fill a large pastry bag with butter cream and use star tip No. 15. Pipe the rosettes in a circular motion, one at a time — if you try to pipe them continuously, they will turn into scrolls.

Simple decorating techniques can produce attractive results — the cake ABOVE is decorated with a serrated comb and piped rosettes.

Swirling

1 You can use a cake comb to create all sorts of patterns in butter icing. Hold the comb against the side of the cake as you rotate it on a turntable, or move it from left to right across the top to make waves, as here.

2 Pipe stars round the edge of the cake and finish it off with a white satin ribbon.

Grooving

1 Use a cake comb with chocolate butter cream to create this complicated looking effect very simply. Rotate the cake on a turntable and move the comb sideways to make undulations. Be careful when you get back to the beginning of your pattern not to make a ridge. Use a deeply grooved comb on the sides of the cake.

2 Pipe a rosette in the centre, and beading around the top and bottom edges of the cake.

Always make a generous quantity of butter cream when decorating cakes like this one ABOVE. A lot of butter cream is scraped off as the pattern is made.

Feather icing

Feathing is an attractive way of finishing off glacé icing or fondant. Fondant is used here. It takes slightly longer to set and gives you more time to work.

1 Pour the fondant over the top of the cake. The cake can have a marzipan base. Pipe straight lines of chocolate icing, fondant or melted chocolate across the cake. The best way of keeping the lines parallel is by working from the centre outwards. Starting at the centre of the cake, draw a skewer through the lines in the opposite direction, leaving a double space between the lines. Turn the cake round and repeat the process in the other direction creating a feather pattern.

2 Roll the sides of the cake in green coloured coconut and pipe a line of chocolate shells round the edge of the cake for a richer effect.

To colour coconut as for the cobweb-iced cake ABOVE, rub a little food colour on to your fingers and work them through the coconut. This method gives a good even colour.

Cobweb icing

1 Pour the fondant over the top of the cake. Pipe concentric circles of chocolate icing, fondant or melted chocolate on the fondant. Start from the centre and work outwards. When the circles are completed, draw a skewer across the cake from the centre outwards, dividing it into quarters. Draw the skewer from the edge of the cake inwards, dividing it into eighths.

2 Hold the cake in the palms of your hands and roll the sides in green coloured coconut.

DECORATING ROLLS

Cylindrical cakes can either be made with sponge cake batter and rolled up (see p.20) or with fruit batter baked in a cylindrical pan.

Yule log

This traditional Yule log decoration makes a simple, but attractive Christmas cake.

1 To make the ends of the log look like sawn wood, roll out a thin square of creamy yellow fondant icing and brush it with brown food colour diluted in water. Cut the icing into strips. Join the strips up into a continuous length and roll the length up.

2 With a very sharp knife, cut two thin slices off the roll. Set the roll aside.

3 Flatten the slices to merge the strips into one, and create a pattern of age rings as in the trunk of a tree. Cut the circles to size to fit the ends of the cake.

4 Fix the circles to the ends of the cake with chocolate butter cream. Cover the sides of the cake with butter cream and run the back of a fork along the surface to create a bark effect.

5 For the sawn-off branches, roll a fat sausage of brown marzipan about 2cm/ ¾in thick. Cut the ends off at 90 degrees to the roll and then cut it in two with a diagonal cut.

6 Position the diagonal ends in the butter cream. Cut two small circles from the fondant icing roll to cover the ends of the branches. Cover the branches with butter cream and use the back of a fork to create bark as before.

7 Finish the decoration with a robin and an axe and sprinkle the cake with sifted icing sugar for a snowy effect.

Swiss roll

1 Cover the Swiss roll with butter cream, taking it down the sides. Leave the underside and the ends uncovered.

2 Dip the sides of the cake in chocolate sprinkles and either pipe ridges along the top with a fine tip or mark ridges with a fork.

3 Pipe a line of shells across the centre of the cake and decorate it with walnuts, cherries and angelica.

The ridges on this decorated Swiss roll ABOVE can either be piped or marked with a small fork.

Chapter Three:
MOULDING AND
MODELLING

Choosing and making decorations is an important part of cake decorating. Whether they are an integral part of the design or added at the last moment as a finishing touch, they must look right on the cake and not spoil the effect by being out of proportion or made from the wrong material.

This section demonstrates several different ways of making decorations, as well as showing how to paint decorations on cakes with food colour and illustrating a selection of items from the bewildering range of ready-made edible and inedible decorations. Edible decorations can be made from marzipan, fondant icing, gelatin icing, modelling or petal paste, sugar and meringue mixes or chocolate. Different effects are achieved with each. Choose a material which you find easy to work with and which is appropriate to your cake. You may want to incorporate some of the ideas featured here into your own designs or you may like to make them as extra items for a festive occasion.

Edible decorations

The decorations illustrated here are all edible, and are just some of the enormous range of ready-made cake decorations available from both specialist and non-specialist sources.

1 Sugar Christening cradle
2 Sugar stork
3 Sugar vase containing artificial heather sprays
4 Selection of corner leaves and decorations
5 Selection of zinnias
6 Multi-coloured six-petal narcissi
7 Selection of wafer roses and leaves
8 Sugar pansies
9 Sugar violets
10 Assorted sugar flowers
11 Small sugar blossoms
12 Sugar 'stick-on' pre-formed flower candle holders
13 Sugar 'stick-on' pre-formed lettering
14 Selection of sugar novelties

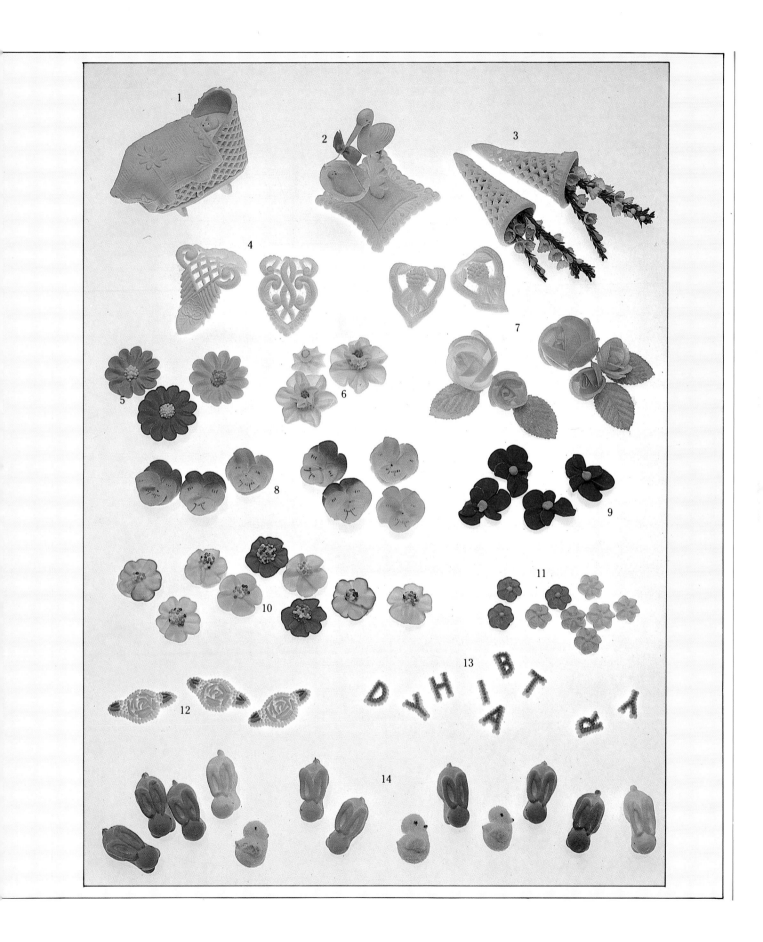

MOULDING ICINGS

FONDANT ICING

This is not as complicated to prepare as at first seems, and it does keep fresh for several months. If you make a large quantity it will always be on hand when you need it. Half the quantity is enough to cover a 21–24cm/8½–9½in cake.

The fondant must be softened before use. Place the amount you need in a heat-proof bowl and set it over a pan half-filled with simmering water; in this instance the water may come up the sides of the bowl. Warm very gently and add just a little tepid water (about 2tbsp is enough for 9oz fondant), for an unperfumed flavour. When the fondant mixture has the texture of thick cream it is ready for instant use.

To colour the fondant, add a drop of vegetable colouring. For a spirituous flavour, use kirsch, dark rum or Grand Marnier instead of the water.

Strained lemon or orange juice gives a good citrus tang, while 2tsp coffee extract or 1tbsp instant coffee dissolved in 1tsp boiling water gives coffee flavouring. For chocolate flavour add 2tbsp cocoa powder, or melt 40g/1½oz chocolate and mix it with the thinned fondant. Fondant handles in much the same way as glacé icing. See pages 68–9 for the method of applying the icing to a cake.

Ingredients

For 500g/1lb icing
165ml/5½fl oz/⅔ cup water
450g/1lb/2 cups sugar
½tsp lemon juice, strained

1 Pour the water into a heavy-based pan, add the sugar and lemon juice. Heat gently until the sugar has dissolved, then bring to the boil and cook briskly until the syrup reaches the soft ball stage (115°C/240°F); 2–3 minutes of boiling. Pour the hot sugar syrup on to a cold damp marble slab or wet work-top and leave to cool for 1 minute.

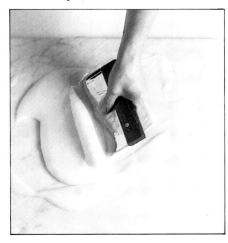

5 The texture, too, becomes thicker.

2 Using a wooden spatula or metal
scraper, work all round the syrup, lifting
it from the edges and slapping and folding it
over into the middle.

3 The syrup starts by being clear and
transparent.

4 Slowly it becomes a dense, creamy mass.

6 Continue using the spatula or scraper
while the syrup is too hot to handle.

7 The syrup will set hard if your don't
continue to work it. Once the mixture is
thick and cool enough, start to work it by
hand.

8 Continue kneading and punching the
mixture: after about 10 minutes it
should look matt white and feel smooth and
firm. Wrap in a plastic wrap and leave to rest
for 1 hour, or store in the refrigerator.

SATIN ICING

This is very similar to easy fondant icing, but the fat content gives it a particularly smooth finish, hence its name. The quantity given is sufficient to cover a 23cm/9in cake.

Ingredients

50g/2oz/4tbsp butter, margarine or white fat (shortening)
2tbsp lemon juice
2tbsp water
about 675g/1½lb/about 4½–5 cups icing sugar, sifted
few drops edible food colouring (optional)

Method

1 Put the fat and liquids in a saucepan and heat gently until the fat has melted. Add about one-third of the sugar and stir over a low heat until dissolved. Increase the heat slightly and cook until the mixture just begins to boil. Remove from the heat.

2 Stir in another one-third of the sugar and beat well until evenly mixed. Turn the mixture into a mixing bowl.

3 Add sufficient of the remaining sugar to mix to a firm paste. Dust the work surface with icing sugar and knead the icing until smooth.

4 Add a few drops of food colouring, if wished, and knead well until evenly coloured. Wrap in a polythene bag or cling film, and place in an airtight plastic container. The icing will keep for several weeks in the refrigerator. To use, allow to soften at room temperature and knead until smooth.

MALLOW PASTE

This icing sets firm and is particularly good for modelling or moulding flowers. The quantity given is sufficient to cover an 18cm/7in cake.

Ingredients

2tsp gelatine
2tsp white fat
3tbsp water
500g/1lb 2oz/about 3½ cups icing sugar, sifted
edible food colouring (optional)

Method

1 Place the gelatine, fat and water in a bowl over a saucepan of simmering water and heat gently until dissolved.

2 Pour mixture over three-quarters of the sugar in a bowl and work together with fingertips until a smooth paste is formed, adding as much of the remaining sugar as necessary. Colour as wished and store as for satin icing.

GELATINE ICING

Gelatine icing is mainly used for modelling work, as an alternative to modelling paste or petal paste.

When you are ready to start using the icing, work with it quickly, as it sets rapidly and shaping can become difficult even after a minute. Always keep the icing you are not using tightly wrapped in plastic wrap.

Ingredients

55ml/2fl oz/¼ cup water
2 envelopes unflavoured gelatine powder
2tsp golden syrup
450g/1lb/3⅓ cups icing sugar, sifted
cornflour

Colouring gelatine icing
If the icing is to be coloured, the colour can be added to the warm gelatine mixture making it easier to incorporate into the icing. However, adding the colour in advance does mean that the colour may be darker than you had expected.

1 Put the water in a small bowl and add the gelatine. Let soak for 2 minutes.

2 Place the bowl in an ovenproof pan containing 1cm/½in of water, and put the pan over direct heat.

3 Heat the water to simmering, stirring constantly until all the lumps have dissolved and the liquid is clear. Remove the bowl from the pan and let cool for 1 minute.

4 Add the golden syrup to the gelatine mixture and stir until dissolved. Let cool for 2 minutes.

5 Place the sugar in a mixing bowl, then add the gelatine mixture and stir with a wooden spoon. If the mixture is a little wet, add more powdered sugar.

6 Stir sufficient cornflour in to the mixture in order to allow the icing to be worked like bread dough.

7 To store the icing, wrap it tightly in a plastic bag. Any air coming into contact with the surface of the icing will cause it to get dry and hard, making it impossible to use.

MODELLING PASTE

This recipe includes icing sugar, edible gums and other edible materials which impart flexibility and elasticity to the paste. Gum tragacanth is available from specialist cake decorating sources.

Ingredients

2tsp gelatine
5tsp cold water
450g/1lb/2¾ cups icing sugar, sifted
1tbsp gum tragacanth
2tsp light golden syrup
2tsp white fat
1 egg white

Method

1 Soak the gelatine in the cold water for about half an hour. Meanwhile, heat the icing sugar and gum tragacanth in a bowl over a pan of warm water.

2 Add the golden syrup and white fat to the gelatine and dissolve over very low heat.

3 Beat the sugar mixture in an electric mixer at a slow speed. Add the golden syrup mixture and the egg white. Turn the machine to maximum speed and beat for about 15 minutes. The longer and harder you beat the paste, the whiter it will be.

PETAL PASTE

Petal paste is made simply by adding water to a special gum powder available from specialist cake decorating sources.

Ingredients

1½tbsp water
450g/1lb/2¾ cups petal paste powder
½tsp white fat (optional)

1 Put the water into a bowl. Sift in most of the petal paste powder. Always use water and powder in the ratio of 1:10.

2 Sift the remaining powder on to the work surface. Work the contents of the bowl into a thick paste, then cover the bowl and let stand for 5 minutes to allow the gum to activate. Scrape the contents of the bowl out on to the counter.

3 Knead the paste until the rest of the powder is incorporated. This creates a smooth pliable paste. For greater elasticity, knead the white fat into the paste.

4 The paste may be used immediately, but it is best left for 24 hours. Store the paste in an airtight container.

COATING CAKES

Coating with marzipan for fondant icing

If you intend to finish your cake with fondant rather than royal icing, a slightly different technique is involved. The marzipan needs to be rounded at the corners and edges, because the fondant is applied to the top and sides of the cake in one process. Use warm beaten apricot jam or lightly beaten egg white to hold the marzipan in position.

Fondant icing does not become discoloured by marzipan in the way that royal icing does, so either natural or coloured marzipan can be used.

1 Turn the cake upside down, so that the flatter surface becomes the top. Trim the sides if necessary and fill any holes with marzipan dampened with lightly beaten egg white. Roll a long, thin sausage of marzipan, paint the edge of the base of the cake with lightly beaten egg white and attach marzipan.

2 Press the marzipan on to the cake with a metal spatula to secure it. Do not use your fingers.

4 Roll out a square of marzipan large enough to cover the top and sides of the cake, allowing for some surplus.

5 Pick up the marzipan right-side up. Use your right hand to pick up the marzipan and slide it over your left hand. Drape it over the cake.

7 Once the top is flat, flare out the corners. Make sure you do not stretch the marzipan too much, or it will crack and craze. Smooth and fit the corners using the palm of your hand before you fit the sides. Make sure the sides are flat and not pleated or creased.

8 Use the warmth of your hand to help smooth off the marzipan and ensure it is well fixed to the cake.

3 Turn the cake the right way up and place it on a sheet of wax paper. Moisten the cake all over with lightly beaten egg white.

6 Hold the marzipan up from beneath with one hand and smooth it down with the other towards the raised hand to exclude air bubbles.

9 With a metal spatula trim the marzipan to the base of the cake making a neat edge all the way around.

Coating a round cake with fondant

Prepare the cake by glazing with boiled apricot jam and/or coating with marzipan (see below). Melt the fondant in a double boiler and add stock syrup to thin it down if necessary.

1 Stand the cake on a wire rack and pour the fondant carefully on to the centre of it. Give it a fairly thick coating so that it will run over the sides of the cake. The excess will drip through the mesh of the rack.

2 Use a metal spatula to smooth over the top and sides of the cake. Tap the wire rack a few times on the counter to settle the icing. As it settles, it will drip off the base. It is important to use a wire rack, so that the fondant does not build up at the bottom of the cake and spoil its shape.

Coating a square cake with fondant

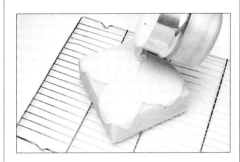

1 Prepare the fondant as for a round cake, and stand the square cake on a wire rack. Pour the fondant over the cake from corner to corner in a diagonal cross.

2 Use the metal spatula to push the fondant from the centre of the cake to the sides and down the edges, working fairly fast before it starts to set. Tap the wire rack to settle the fondant and dislodge any air bubbles.

PASTILLAGE

Moulded flowers

This section shows you how to make a spray of tiny flowers, a larger single flower, a briar rose and an azalea. You could make all these flowers with fondant icing or marzipan, but as these tend to spoil in damp or humid conditions, it is better to use modelling or petal paste (see pages 66–7).

Remember when you are working with the petals not to let them dry out completely before you finish molding and shaping, or they will break as you try to put the flower together.

Egg white and water can both be used to fix petals into position on the flower. Egg white forms a stronger bond, but in most cases, water should be sufficient. If the petals are left to dry, or should break off and need replacing, then they must be attached with royal icing. Be very careful not to paint any egg white on to any part of the flower that will show, because it will dry shiny. If you make any mistakes with water, they will not be visible.

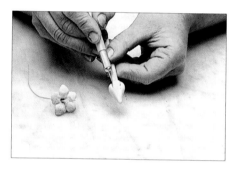
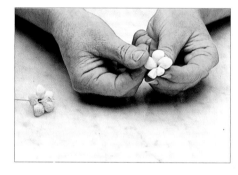

Single bloom

1 Form a cone of petal paste approximately 0.75cm/¼in long and 0.5cm/½in across the base.

2 Push the point of a wooden skewer up into the wide base of the cone. Using a fine sharp knife, cut five even petals around the base of the cone, turning the skewer as you work.

3 Take out the skewer and turn the flower out into your fingers, in order to pull out the petals. Flatten each petal between thumb and forefinger and pull from underneath with your finger against your thumb, flattening and broadening the petal at the same time.

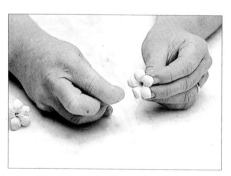

4 For the stalk, make a small hook at the end of a piece of covered wire, dampen the hooked end in water or beaten egg white and pull it through the centre of the flower, hooking into the side of the flower.

5 Cut the stamen in half, dampen the cut ends, and push them into the cente of the soft paste. As it hardens, it will hold them in position. Let dry in an upright position.

6 The result is a perfect flower that you can dust or paint to whatever shade you want.

Briar rose

1 To make a briar or Christmas rose, you will need a shallow curved container to set the flowers in. Bottle tops, a paint palette (as here) or polystyrene fruit trays from the supermarket are all ideal.

To make the calyxes, colour a little petal paste green. Cut out the shapes with a calyx cutter – or you can make your own with a template. Put the template on the petal paste and cut round it with a fine sharp knife. Line the base of each container with a small square of wax paper to prevent the petal paste from sticking and lay the calyxes on top. The calyx will curve to the shape of the container you put it in.

2 Cut five small circles for petals from pink petal paste using a plain round cutter 0.75cm/¼in in diameter and lay them on foam rubber. Curl the petals with a modelling tool, such as the dog bone, by running it gently along the edge of the petal, half on the petal and half on the foam. A delicately frilled edge will result. To curve the petal, indent the base with the ball tool or your little finger, by pushing down into the foam rubber. Pull the end of the petal out to elongate it slightly.

3 Paint inside the calyx with water or lightly beaten egg white and position the first petal carefully.

4 Brush one side of the petal lightly with lightly beaten egg white or water and leave the other side free (the fifth petal will be tucked underneath it). Lay the second petal in place overlapping the painted edge and continue until four petals are in position. Slip the fifth petal in under the edge of the first. Paint the underside of the first to secure them in place.

5 To make the centre of the flower, roll a very small ball of yellow paste and press it into a fine piece of tulle, so that the weave of the fabric is imprinted on the paste, giving the effect of stamens. This technique can also be used in making a daisy. Position in the centre of the flower and adhere with beaten egg white or water.

6 Cut a few stamens about 0.5cm/¼in long and insert them into the centre of the flower with a pair of tweezers. The end result is a very authentic-looking briar rose. Briar roses make very attractive decorations for royal-iced celebration cakes.

Flower sprays

1 It is important to roll out pastillage as thinly as possible. Put a piece of paste the size of a large pea on a smooth work surface that you have lightly dusted with icing sugar or cornflour or a mixture of both. Remember that cornflour is a drying agent, so use it very sparingly. Use a stainless steel rolling pin.

Each time the paste is rolled, lift the paste with a metal spatula to ensure that it does not stick to the counter. Roll the paste out so that it is thin enough to read through when you lay it on a printed page.

2 Plunger cutters are very useful gadgets for making petal paste flowers. Press the cutter into the paste and give it a gentle twist.

3 Lift the cutter together with the cut flower and, holding the cutter on a piece of foam rubber, depress the plunger. As it is pushed into the foam, the paste will be cupped and will form the shape of a flower. You can use a cutter without a plunger, in which case push the flower out of the cutter with a paintbrush.

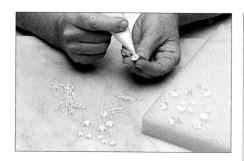

4 To wire the flowers into a spray, prick a hole in the centre of each one with a thick needle. Do this before they have dried or they will break.

5 Stamens come with a knob at each end, so cut them in half and double the number. To insert a stamen, put it into the hole in the flower and pull it halfway through. Letting the flower rest on your fingertips, squeeze a little royal icing from a bag (you do not need a tip) into the base of the flower and pull the stamen gently down into it. Turn the flowers upside down to dry.

6 To make a bud using a stamen as its base, take a tiny amount of paste, flatten it between finger and thumb and roll it up round the stamen. Dampen the tip of the stamen in lightly beaten egg white or water first so that the paste will stick.

7 To attach flowers and buds to a spray, use white floristry tape. Take a 10cm/4in strip and cut it in half widthways. Stretch it out until it is about four times its original length.

8 Lay the tape along your index finger and roll the wire stalk into the tape. Start arranging your spray. Put one or two buds at the top of the wire, catching the last 0.5cm/¼in of the stamen bases in the tape with the wire as you turn it.

9 Start adding the flowers one by one and, as you roll the tape around the stalk, catching the base of the stamens, the tape will travel down the wire so that each flower is slightly lower than the preceding one.

10 Use five to seven flowers to a spray. Finish by completely covering the wire with the tape, then cut the stalk off to a length of about 5cm/2in.

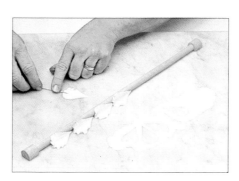

Azalea

1 To make an azalea you need a piece of dowelling or a similar prop to fold the petals against. With a teardrop shaped cutter, or with a template, cut out five petals from the paste. Cover the petals you are not working on with plastic. Gently mark the centre vein of the petal with a wooden pick and two on either side. Be careful not to press too heavily or you will slice through the petal. These marks will not really show until you come to colour the flower.

2 To create a frilled edge to the petal, roll the wooden pick along the edge of the paste, thinning it to 0.5cm/¼in. Dust the work surface with icing sugar or cornflour. Roll the petal with the left index finger. Line up each petal as it is finished against the dowelling to curve it.

3 To set the petals into a flower shape you will need a small cone – a little medicine funnel is ideal. Line it with wax paper or foil to stop the flower from sticking in the funnel. Drop the first petal into the funnel, paint half the length of one side with lightly beaten egg white or water and put the next petal in position overlapping the painted edge.

4 To secure the petals in position press them gently together with the handle of the paintbrush. Continue until you have four petals in position. The fifth petal will form the azalea's tongue. Nick off the point and drop it in over the first and fourth petals.

5 Pipe a tiny spot of royal icing from a bag into the throat of the flower and, with a pair of tweezers, insert seven stamens, six of equal length and one longer for the pistil. Leave the flower to dry. Once the flower is completely dry, you can paint it with food colours or dust it with petal dust. Put a little cotton into the cup of the flower so that the petal dust touches only the edges. Brush from the outside inwards to get a graduated effect. Paint little spots on the tongue of the azalea.

The petal dust gives the finished azaleas a sheen.

MAKING MOULDED ROSES

Making a moulded rose requires patience and a steady hand. The rose shown below is made with fondant icing. You can also use marzipan, though its slightly grainier texture means that the petals are less fine.

Moulding fine shapes like petals with fondant icing or marzipan can be a problem if your hands and fingers get hot, because the fondant or marzipan will stick to them. There are two ways of preventing this. Either dust your fingers very lightly with cornflour, or mould the petals inside a plastic bag. If you use the cornflour method, make sure you use only a very little.

1 Roll a ball of fondant icing the size of an egg in the heels of your hands until it forms a cone about 5cm/2in high and put it point upwards on your counter.

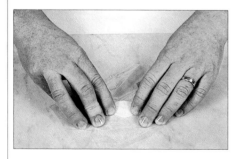

2 To make each petal, follow the same technique. Roll a ball of fondant about the size of a large pea. Put it in a plastic bag or under a sheet of plastic.

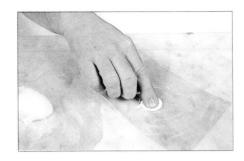

3 Squash it with your index finger. Using both index fingers, flatten the paste at the top edge to form the edge of the petal. The base of the petal should remain thick so that it can be attached to the flower. Another way to mould the petals, if you have cool hands, is to stroke and pull the edge of the petal between your fingers, or lay the petal on the palm of one hand and flatten and thin it with a ball tool.

4 Wrap the first petal right around the cone with the top fo the petal 0.5cm/¼in above the top fo the cone. You should not need water to adhere the petals to the cone.

5 Gently squeeze it in with your fingers to form a 'waist' at the bottom of the petal. The first petal should be completely closed around the cone.

6 Place the centre edge of the second petal opposite the joint line of the first petal and 0.5cm/¼in above it. Attach one side of the petal firmly to the cone. Curl the tips of the petal back – do not wait too long to do this or the fondant will dry and crack.

7 Place the centre of the third petal over the closed side of the second petal. Attach it on both sides of the cone and curl the tip back.

8 Place the centre of the fourth petal over the edge of the third and under the open side of the second. Close the edge of the second petal down. Curl the edge of the fourth petal back.

9 With four petals pinched in neatly at the base, the three outer ones curled back at the tips, you have formed a rosebud. If you wish to stop at this stage, look at the flower from all angles, decide which is the best, and cut the bud from the cone at a slant, so that it will rest on the cake with the best side up.

10 To make a bigger rose, continue to build up the flower with slightly larger petals. It does not matter where you start attaching the outer petals. Stretch the base of each petal round as you secure it to the cone. Apply each petal so that it overlaps the previous one about halfway and curl the tips outwards.

11 Continue adding petals until the rose is fairly even and you have an attractive flower.

12 Turn the rose, gently pressing down each of the petals to ensure they are secured firmly at the base.

13 Cut the base of the rose so that it will stand upright on the cake. Angle the base of each rose carefully according to its position in the final arrangement.

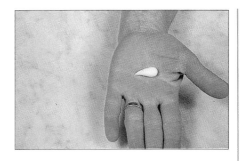

14 To make a very small bud, roll a tiny cone shape on your palm into a rosebud shape.

15 Make one petal, wrap it round the cone and pinch it at the base to form a bud.

These very attractive moulded roses are ideal for use on wedding cakes.

EDIBLE DECORATIONS

Sparkling sugar bells make a very attractive decoration on casually iced cakes, covered with frosting or peaked royal icing. They can be made well in advance and stored for several months very successfully.

Sugared or crystallized flowers also make a very pretty decoration on all kinds of cakes. Choose strong-coloured flowers with a distinctive shape, such as violets, roses and primroses, as the sugar tends to soften the outline. Make sure the flowers are fresh and free from damage or brown marks.

CRYSTALLIZED FLOWERS

Ingredients

15g/¹/₂oz/1tbsp gum arabic
2tbsp rose water
caster sugar
fresh violets

Method

1 Mix together the gum arabic and rose water and leave for about 2 hours or until the gum arabic has dissolved. Stir occasionally.

2 Using a fine artist's paintbrush carefully paint the petals of the flower on both sides. Leave for 15-20 minutes to allow the solution to be absorbed.

SUGAR BELLS

Ingredients

Makes about 20 small bells
50g/2oz/¹/₄ cup granulated sugar
a little royal icing
silver dragées

1 Mix the sugar with a few drops of water, making sure that the sugar is only *just* moistened. Pack the sugar in clean metal bell decorations and level the ends with the back of a knife.

2 Tap out on to a piece of non-stick paper on a baking sheet. Repeat until the sugar is used up.

3 Sprinkle with caster sugar until evenly coated and shake off any excess. Place on a sheet of non-stick paper on a baking sheet and leave to dry in a warm place for 1–2 days. Remove carefully and store in an airtight tin, between layers of tissue paper.

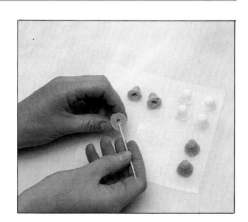

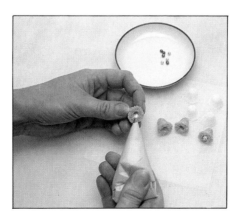

3 Leave until the sugar on the outside of the bells is hardened and you can pick them up without breaking them. Carefully scrape out the soft centres with a skewer to leave a bell-shaped shell. Leave overnight until completely dried out.

4 Pipe a line of icing from the centre of the inside of each bell to the edge and stick a silver dragée at the end for a clapper. Leave until set. The sugar bells may be stored in an airtight container between layers of tissue paper until required.

Sugar mice

1 To make sugar mice, mix granulated sugar with lightly beaten egg white or water as for the sugar bells. Leave half the mixture white and colour the other half pink and pack solidly into the moulds. Turn the mice out on to wax paper.

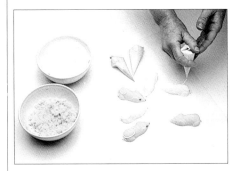

2 Make their tails with pieces of string, thin sausages of fondant icing or pipe them with royal icing. Pipe pink eyes and noses for the white mice and chocolate features for the pink mice. The same moulds can also be used for marzipan, chocolate or fondant mice.

Meringue mushrooms

1 First make a meringue mixture and, using tip No. 3 or 4, pipe the stems of the mushrooms, bringing them up to a point. Make them flat at the bottom, so that they do not topple over when assembled. Pipe little beads or circles for the caps of the mushrooms. Pull the tip gently to the side to remove it, instead of pulling it up, or it will make a point. If you do get a point, however, push it down with a dampened finger and it will disappear.

2 Sprinkle the mushroom tops with sifted cocoa and bake on a baking sheet covered with wax paper in a very cool oven for an hour or two. To test if they are done, tap them lightly with your finger. They should sound hollow and lift easily off the paper.

3 To assemble the mushrooms, make a tiny hollow under the cap with your little finger or a ball tool. Push the stem into the cap and stand them up.

Easter eggs

1 To make these miniature Easter egg decorations, make sure the mould is perfectly clean.

2 Make sure that the chocolate is not too hot, then pour it — either from a spoon or a saucepan — into the mould. Fill the mould all the way to the edge.

3 Leave the mould until the eggs are ready to be released. As the chocolate begins to release from the mould by itself, it will turn slightly opaque. Turn the mould upside down and the eggs will fall out.

4 Let the eggs dry completely, then cover them with different colours of royal icing.

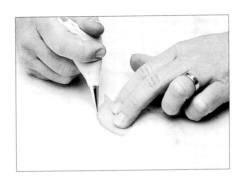

Leaves

1 Cut a paper pattern for the leaf shape you require. Pin it to a piece of green tulle and cut round the tulle to the shape of your pattern.

2 Place the tulle leaf on a strip of wax paper and pipe round the edge with green royal icing. A delicate scalloped edge is shown, but you can pipe a shell border or a snail trail — as long as it hides the cut edge of the leaf.

3 Pipe the centre vein and the smaller veins at the side with pale green royal icing and a fine tip.

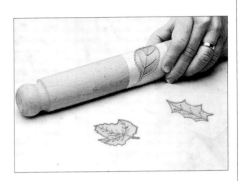

4 If you want to make the leaf curl, secure a rolling pin to the counter by placing a small ball of icing under each end. Before the leaf dries, curl it on its wax paper round the rolling pin. Stick the paper to the rolling pin with two dabs of icing. You can make all kinds of leaves in this way, to use among floral decorations.

When the chocolate Easter eggs are dry, decorations can be piped on them with coloured icing and a very fine tip.

DECORATING WITH CHOCOLATE

Melted chocolate can be used very effectively to decorate a cake and several ideas are shown here. No doubt you will think of many others as you experiment.

Chocolate decorations can give a really professional finish to any cake. Small decorations can be piped on to non-stick paper, left to set, then carefully peeled off and transferred to the cake. Run-outs can be made in a similar way to that described for royal icing (pages 122-5).

Many of these decorations can also be piped freehand on to a cake. Practise first on a plate – the chocolate can be collected up and remelted. Do remember to let the chocolate cool as much as possible before piping it.

Most chocolate decorations can be made in advance and kept for several weeks in a rigid airtight container, between sheets of greaseproof or waxed, or non-stick paper. Store in a cool place or the refrigerator.

To melt chocolate
Place some broken pieces of chocolate in a small bowl over a saucepan of simmering water until melted. Do not use more heat than is necessary and stir as little as possible.

To pipe melted chocolate
Make a small paper piping bag (pages 16-17) and pour the chocolate directly into it. Fold in the sides and fold over the top to seal it. Snip off a tiny piece at the tip and pipe directly on to the iced cake, or pipe shapes and designs on to non-stick paper.

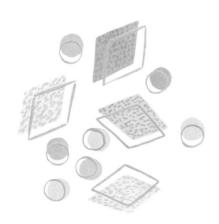

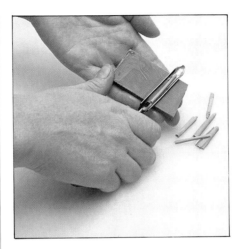

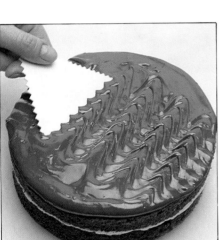

Easy chocolate curls

Use a vegetable peeler to scrape curls from a chocolate bar.

Chocolate caraque

Melt some chocolate and spread evenly on a piece of marble or plastic laminate. Leave to set. Using a sharp knife held at a 45 degree angle to the chocolate, scrape the knife away from you across the surface of the chocolate to make long chocolate curls. This takes some practice, but produces superior curls. Ragged edged petals can be made by using a small sharp knife and rotating it over the surface of the chocolate.

Combed chocolate

This is done directly on to the cake. Spread the surface of the cake with melted chocolate and when beginning to firm, use an icing comb or folk to produce a pattern. Draw the comb across the chocolate in straight or wavy lines.

Chocolate shapes

These are made from melted chocolate that has been spread thinly and left to harden.

Melt the chocolate. Secure a piece of non-stick paper to a baking sheet with a dab of chocolate, then spread the chocolate evenly. Tap the tray to level the surface of the chocolate, then leave in a cool place (not the refrigerator) to set.

When just set, stamp out shapes using warmed cutters, or cut squares, triangles and other shapes freehand with a warm sharp knife. Leave until completely firm. Gently ease off the paper with a palette knife, then store until required.

Contrasting chocolate may be piped on these shapes to give a more decorative finish.

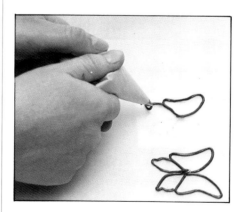

Chocolate run-outs

1 Draw a template of the required shape and place it under a square of non-stick paper so that the outline shows through. Pipe the outline in chocolate and allow it to set.

2 Carefully fill the centre of the outline with melted chocolate, easing it into the corners with a skewer or cocktail stick. Tap the tray gently on the work surface to remove any ridges from the chocolate. Leave to set completely, then carefully remove from the paper and store. For butterflies 'in flight', fold the non-stick paper along the 'body line'. After piping, leave to set, supported at a 90-degree angle, in a small square container.

Chocolate cones

1 Make tiny non-stick paper cones, from 10cm/4in squares, in the same way as you would make a piping bag. Using an artist's paintbrush, brush the inside of each cone with chocolate. Leave to set.

2 Paint a second coat of chocolate for added strength. Leave to set, then carefully peel away the paper.

3 If you wish to level the top edge of the cone, very carefully press it on to a just warm cake tin or baking sheet. The cones may be filled with fresh cream or butter cream.

Chocolate leaves

1 Wash and dry rose leaves or fresh bay leaves. Paint the undersurface of each leaf with melted chocolate and leave to set, chocolate side up.

2 Carefully peel away the leaf and you will be left with a chocolate replica.

Chopped or grated chocolate

Finely chop or grate the chocolate on a coarse grater.

MAKING MARZIPAN

Marzipan is most often used as the 'undercoat' icing for a rich fruit cake. It can, however, be used on its own as an icing for fruit cakes or plain cakes, or as an 'undercoat' icing on sponge cakes which are to be covered in fondant or other mouldings icings.

It is made from ground almonds, sugar and egg. The egg may be whole, beaten egg, or egg yolks or egg whites. It is perhaps more usual to use egg yolks only as the whites can then be kept to make other icings. Using egg whites does give a paler colour, which is more useful if colourings are to be added for decorating purposes.

Commercially made marzipan is available in blocks. Knead this well, adding a little egg, if necessary, to soften it to a suitable consistency. Use as a convenient alternative to homemade.

Almond paste contains a lot of oil and it must be allowed to dry completely before a white icing is used as a covering. Allow about one week before applying royal icing. The quantity given in the basic recipe makes about 900g/2lb almond paste.

COATING WITH MARZIPAN FOR ROYAL ICING

A common problem with cakes covered in marzipan and then royal icing is that the icing becomes discoloured by the marzipan beneath. This happens usually because there is too much oil in the marzipan and it has not been allowed to dry thoroughly before being covered with icing. Allow the cake plenty of time to dry and use a cooked, not uncooked, marzipan.

This problem does not occur with bought marzipan. If possible, choose white or naturally coloured marzipan.

Ingredients

450g/1lb/2⅔ cups ground almonds
450g/1lb caster sugar/2 cups or use half caster and half icing sugar
about 2 eggs, beaten, or 4 egg yolks or whites
2tsp lemon juice
1tsp almond essence

Method

1 Mix the ground almonds and sugar in a large bowl. If using icing sugar, sift it first to remove any lumps.

2 Add three-quarters of the egg with the lemon juice and almond essence, and work to a smooth paste, adding more egg as required.

3 Turn out on to a work surface sprinkled with a little icing sugar and knead until smooth. Wrap in cling film or polythene and store in the refrigerator until required.

Quantities of marzipan required to cover top and sides of round and square cakes.

These quantities allow a generous layer of almond paste; obviously less may be used.

Size of cake	Quantity of almond paste
15cm/6in square 18cm/7in round	450g/1lb
18cm/7in square 20cm/8in round	675g/1½lb
20cm/8in square 23cm/9in round	900g/2lb
23cm/9in square 25cm/10in round	1.2kg/2½lb
25cm/10in square 28cm/11in round	1.4kg/3lb
28cm/11in square 30cm/12in round	1.6kg/3½lb
30cm/12in square	1.8kg/4lb

1 Always turn the cake over to decorate it, so that the flat base becomes the top. What is now the base of the cake may be concave or convex and this should be dealt with. Either slice off the rounded part if it is concave or fill the hollow with marzipan if it is convex.

2 Roll a long, thin sausage of marzipan and stick it round the base of the cake with jam or lightly beaten egg white by pressing it into the cake with a metal spatula. This will both seal the edges of the cake to the cake board and help the cake to keep longer.

6 Turn the cake the right way up, being careful not to leave finger marks in the marzipan. Trim off any excess marzipan from the bottom sausage. Ensure that the sides of the cake are smooth, filling any small holes with pieces of marzipan.

3 Sprinkle the work surface with icing sugar. Roll out the marzipan, using spacers as a guide to even thickness and the right width, which should be a little more than the diameter of the cake.

4 Turn the marzipan over, sprinkling more confectioner's sugar beneath it if necessary. The smoother, rolled side of the marzipan is the 'right' side. Brush a circle of warm apricot jam or lightly beaten egg white the same size as the diameter of the cake on the 'wrong' side of the marzipan. Alternatively, brush the cake with jam. Apricot is generally used rather than other jams because it does not dominate the flavour of the marzipan.

5 Place the cake top down on the marzipan. Cut the marzipan closely round the cake.

7 Roll out a strip of marzipan about 0.5cm/¼in thick for the sides of the cake. The length of the strip should be three times the diameter of the cake. Measure the depth of the strip to fit the sides. Make sure your work surface is well dusted with icing sugar. Turn the marzipan over, so that the smoother side is face down. Brush the marzipan with warm apricot jam or lightly beaten egg white.

8 Roll the cake along the marzipan, pressing it into position. If you have miscalculated, and you need to add a little extra marzipan, ensure the joints are neat.

9 If you are covering a square cake, measure the sides of the cake and cut two pieces to fit. Attach them to opposite sides of the cake and measure the two remaining sides plus the thickness of the marzipan before cutting and fitting.

10 Now the cake is completely covered, smooth it carefully with the heel and palm of your hands. A smooth, flat coating of marzipan will provide the perfect base for a professional icing for the cake.

MARZIPAN FRUITS

Almond paste (marzipan) is a very easy mixture to work with and can be modelled into shapes, such as fruit, or rolled out and stamped with shaped cutters. It absorbs edible food colouring very well, although its basic yellow colour (more pronounced in commercially produced pastes) may distort some colours. For example, purple colouring can result in a greyish finish. However there are now many makes of superior colouring, mainly in paste form, which give very good results.

It is important to make any decorations to a sensible scale for the cake on which they are to be used. Figures and animals will generally require between 25g/1oz and 75g/3oz of paste. Always leave the decorations to dry on non-stick paper for a few days to prevent any oil and colouring seeping through on to white icing. Attach the decorations to the cake with a dab of icing.

Lemon

1 Roll a ball of yellow marzipan, squeezing to give it two slightly pointed ends. Using a ball tool, indent the stalk end.

2 Using the serrated end of modelling tool No. 4, work it over the fruit to give the appearance of lemon peel. Alternatively roll the marzipan lemon around on a nutmeg grater.

Pear

1 Roll out a ball of yellow or green paste. Elongate the ball by rolling one side of it with your finger to form the neck of the pear. Roll your little finger around the base of the neck to form its 'waist'.

2 Use the star tool to form the little indentations at the base and stalk of the pear. You can speckle it with brown marzipan to make it look more authentic.

Strawberry

1 Roll a red ball into a cone shape. Take a 10cm/4in square of fine tulle. Place the strawberry in the centre of the tulle.

2 Draw the tulle up tightly around the marzipan and the fabric pattern will give a strawberry effect. Add a green paste leaf or a plastic culotte if available.

Grapes

For a bunch of grapes, roll a cone of purple or green paste and make several tiny balls to represent the grapes. Arrange the grapes all over the cone to form a bunch, pressing each one gently into position.

Orange

Roll a ball of orange marzipan and use the serrated end of modelling tool No. 4 or a nutmeg grater to give the effect of peel. Use star tool No. 5 to make an indentation for the stem.

Banana

Roll a piece of yellow marzipan into a sausage shape. Curve it with your fingers and flatten the sides to give it a banana shape. Finally, paint or dust on strands of brown food colour to give the banana a ripe appearance.

Apple, plum, apricot, cherry

For an apple, take red or green marzipan and roll it into a ball. Indent the top and tail with tool No. 5. Using appropriate colours make the other fruits in the same way. Use tool No. 2 to give an authentic crease to the fruit. Attach stamens to the cherries to represent stalks.

Finishing touches

1 To finish your fruits, you can dust them with various colours for shading, give them a shine with gum arabic or coat them in sugar.

2 To coat them in sugar, brush a little lightly beaten egg white on to the palm of your hand and roll the fruit in it. This is quicker than painting the fruit and you will get a lighter coat. Roll the fruit in caster sugar to create a very pretty effect.

3 Finally you can use chocolate sprinkles as miniature stems for the fruit. Alternatively, use cloves, but they may be too large. For the orange and the lemon, tiny star-shaped soup noodles can be soaked for a second or two in a weak solution of green food colouring. If you allow them to soak longer, they will swell.

RIGHT: A variety of fruits grouped together makes an attractive decoration for a plain cake.

MARZIPAN ANIMALS

Rabbit

1 Follow guidelines for kangaroo (right) but make pointed ears and a bob tail.

2 Pipe eyes, nose and whiskers with icing.

Cat

1 Reserve a small piece for the tail and roll to a suitable length, divide the remaining paste into two-thirds and one-third.

2 Make an arch as for the body of the elephant (right) and roll the smaller amount into a ball; make a cut half way through the ball to shape the ears.

3 Fasten the pieces together with a little unbeaten egg white and pipe nose, eyes and whiskers with royal icing.

Tiger

1 Use the kangaroo as a guide, but reserve a little paste to make a roll for the tail and make two more small balls which are flattened and marked for the tiger's face.

2 The body and head should be oval. Pipe all over the body and tail with stripes of chocolate as well as piping the eyes.

Mouse

1 Reserve two tiny circles for the ears and pinch together at one end to make a point. Roll a length of paste for a tail.

2 Roll the remaining paste into a pear shape with a pointed end.

3 Attach the pieces together with a little unbeaten egg white. Leave to dry, then pipe eyes, nose and whiskers with royal icing.

Elephant

1 Use about two-thirds of the paste for the body. Roll into a thick cylinder and arch it so that it will stand up.

2 Cut a small indentation at the front and back of the arch to make the legs.

3 Press out two small circles for the ears and a tiny piece for the tail; shape the remaining paste into the head and trunk. Press lines into the trunk with a sharp knife and two holes in the end of the trunk for the nostrils.

4 Fasten the piece together with a little unbeaten egg white and leave to dry. Pipe eyes with chocolate.

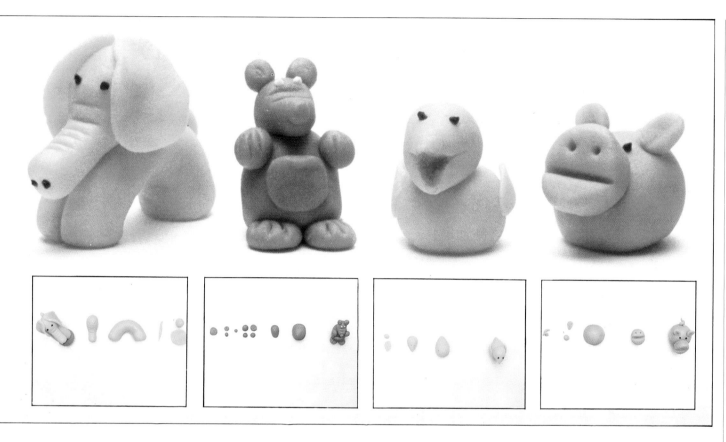

Kangaroo

1 Make three tiny balls: two for ears and one for nose. Make two medium-sized balls for the paws and two slightly larger balls for the feet and one for a tiny pouch.

2 Divide the remaining paste into three-quarters and one-quarter. Roll each into an oval shape for the body and head. Flatten the two feet slightly and mark indentations in each, then attach to the body with a little unbeaten egg white.

3 Mark two horizontal lines on the head; press two small balls to shape the ears and attach to the head. Press the nose into place. Attach the head.

4 Mark indentations on the paws and attach in place. Attach the pouch. Leave to dry, then pipe the eyes with royal icing or chocolate.

Chicken

1 Make two small wings, then divide remaining paste into two-thirds and one-third. Shape each one into an egg shape with a pointed end.

2 Cut a small horizontal line in the point of the smaller ball for the beak. Attach the two pieces with a little unbeaten egg white and paint the inside of the beak orange.

3 Pipe eyes with edible food colouring, royal icing or chocolate. Attach wings.

Pig

1 Roll three-quarters of the paste into a ball. Make two tiny circles for the ears and bring them together at one end to form a point; roll another tiny piece into a curly tail.

2 Use the remaining paste for the snout; shape into a ball, then completely flatten one side. Make two large holes for the nostrils and cut a horizontal line for the mouth.

3 Fasten the pieces together with a little unbeaten egg white and leave to dry. Pipe eyes with a little royal icing or chocolate.

Scottie dog

1 Roll a sausage of dark brown marzipan about 10cm/4in long and 1.5cm/¾in thick. Cut off a quarter for the head and mark the remaining piece to divide it into three.

2 Snip a piece from the top of the rolled marzipan and lift it gently to form the tail. Cut through the sausage from beneath the tail to the end to make the back legs. The front legs are formed in the same way.

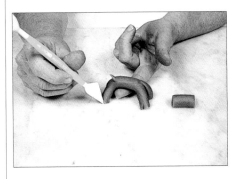

3 Twist the legs apart gently and arch the marzipan to form the dog's body. Adjust the legs so that the dog stands firmly. Mark its paws.

4 Take the head and pinch up two ears with your thumb and forefinger. Indent the ears with the dog bone tool.

5 Pull out the dog's whiskers by stroking with the thumb and forefinger, and snip it into a fringe with the scissors.

6 Press a small ball of pink marzipan between the whiskers with the 'U' tool to form the mouth, and add a red tongue. Make a depression for the nose with tool No. 5 and insert a small cone of black marzipan.

7 Make two indentations for the eyes and fill them with white royal icing. Paint on black dots to complete the eyes.

8 Position the head on the body at an angle and fix it in place. The tam o'shanter cap is made by rolling red and green marzipan together and pressing a red pompom on top. Complete the model by giving the dog a bone.

Goldfish

1 Roll out a sausage of orange marzipan 2.5cm/1in thick and 6cm/2½in long. Make two indentations, one with the little finger very close to one end to form the mouth and the second with the index finger a little further from the other end to form the goldfish's tail.

2 Stroke the marzipan between the thumb and forefinger to form a fin on the top of the fish and press and flatten the other end to form the tail. Turn the tail slightly to one side so that the fish will stay upright. Use the dog bone tool to impress the mouth and make two holes for the eyes with tool No. 5.

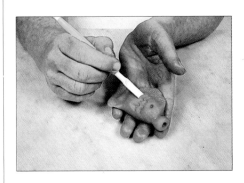

3 With shell tool No. 2, mark the wavy lines on the fins, and use tool No. 4 to mark the scales.

Frog

1 Form a ball of green marzipan 5cm/2in across into a pear shape and flatten and bend it over slightly at the top. Slice through the narrowest part with a sharp knife to form the mouth. Taking about half as much marzipan again, roll a dumb bell shape with one end larger than the other. Roll two smaller balls for the protruding eye sockets.

2 Cut the dumb bell shape in half along its length to make the frog's legs. Twist the smaller end outward to form the foot and mark the webbed feet with tool No. 4.

4 Make the side fins by moulding small cones of marzipan and flattening and curling them into shape. Adhere them to the sides of the fish with beaten egg white. Pipe royal icing for the eyes into the sockets. When the icing is dry, paint black dots to complete the eyes.

Duck

1 Roll four balls of white marzipan, one 5cm/2in across for the body, one 3.5cm/1½in across for the head, and two 1cm/½in across for the wings. Roll two balls of orange marzipan, one 3.5cm/1½in across for the feet and one 0.5cm/¼in across for the beak. Form the large white ball into a cone and drag the tip end of the cone across the work surface to form the uptilted tail. Squeeze the medium-sized white ball gently.

2 Flatten the two smallest white balls into teardrop shapes for the wings. Mark in feathers from the shoulder to the tip with shell tool No. 2. Feathermark the tail in the same way. Elongate the larger orange ball for the feet by forming a depression across the centre.

3 Press out the end of the dumb bell with your thumbs to make the feet. Mark the webs with shell tool No. 2. Roll the other orange ball into a cigar shape and fold in half to form the beak. Pinch the beak up in the middle so that it forms an open 'V' shape.

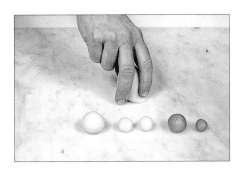

4 Assemble the duck. Adhere the body to the feet with lightly beaten egg white or melted chocolate. Position the beak on the body of the duck and press the head on top, sandwiching the beak between the head and body. Attach the wings with lightly beaten egg white and pipe in the eyes with white royal icing. Mark the eyeballs and eyebrows. Add character with a little hat, and an umbrella made from a cone of marzipan. Slip it between a wing and the body.

3 Attach the legs and eye sockets to the body and make indentations for the eyeballs. Pipe in the eyeballs with white royal icing and complete the eyes with dots of black. Add three small balls of green marzipan to each foot for the toes. Make a few small holes in the frog's back and fill with orange marzipan to make spots. Give the frog a red tongue and adhere a tiny marzipan butterfly to the end of it.

MARZIPAN CHRISTMAS DECORATIONS

These brightly coloured and festive decorations are great fun to make. When you are working with marzipan, keep two cloths handy, one damp and one dry, for cleaning your hands and tools. They get very sticky because of the almond oil. These decorations can also be made from fondant icing.

RIGHT: The complete Christmas decorations will appeal particularly to children.

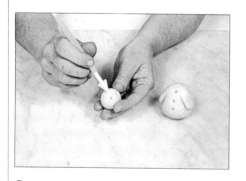

Snowman

1 Make a cone of marzipan or, for a true white snowman, fondant icing. With tool No. 2, the blunt knife, make two upward cuts for arms and lever them out slightly to stand away from the body.

2 Make a ball for the head and make indentations with star tool No. 5 where the eyes, nose and buttons are to be positioned.

3 Push tiny cones of black marzipan into the holes for the eyes and buttons. A very small carrot cone shape makes the nose. A marzipan curl forms the mouth.

4 The scarf is made from a long sausage of marzipan with the ends flattened and snipped to make a fringe. Make the hat by rolling a sausage of marzipan. Cut the ends flat. Make the hat brim by flattening out a little marzipan at the base of the hat between finger and thumb. Make some snowballs and set them beside the finished snowman.

Santa Claus

1 The Santa Claus is rather more complicated and needs overnight drying before assembly. First, roll a 10cm/4in sausage about 1cm/½in thick of red marzipan under the palm of your hand. Do not use your fingers because they will leave indentations on the sausage.

2 Flatten the ends of the sausage and turn them up to form feet. Bow the sausage for the legs. Stand the legs up and let them dry.

3 Make a cone for the body, indenting the base of the cone where the legs will be filled in.

4 Make the arms from a 10cm/4in sausage about 0.5cm/¼in thick and at both ends cut the thumbs with tool No. 2. Smooth them off. Indent the palms with tool No. 2.

5 Roll two equal-sized balls of marzipan for the head, one flesh coloured and one red. Cut each of them in half and sandwich a red one for the hat on to a pink one for the face. You will not need the spare halves.

6 Make a groove for the brow with tool No. 2. Make two indentations for the eye sockets. Use two tiny flattened balls of black marzipan for the eyes.

7 Cut out the trimmings — the belt, beard, eyebrows and fur — with a knife. Stick the trimmings to the head body, arms and legs with lightly beaten egg white. Let all the pieces dry.

8 The next day, assemble the body by threading the legs, body and head on to a wooden pick or piece of uncooked spaghetti. Make a sackful of presents for the finishing touch.

Christmas tree

1 Form a cone of green marzipan. Take a very sharp pair of embroidery scissors and, starting at the top of the cone, snip small 'V' shapes into the marzipan to form branches.

2 Lift each 'V' slightly as you withdraw the scissors to make the branches stand out. Continue snipping all round the tree until it is full of branches. You can use the same technique to make marzipan hedgehogs.

3 Let the tree dry out thoroughly, then give it a seasonal touch of snow by sifting a little icing sugar over the branches.

Holly

1 Roll out a sheet of green marzipan on a smooth work surface lightly dusted with icing sugar. Use a holly cutter if you have one or make a template from the illustration and cut round it with a fine sharp knife.

2 Alternatively, use a small circular cutter, such as the end of a piping tip, and cut a series of circles in an oval shape, the sides of each circle touching the next to form the indentation of the leaf.

3 As you cut the leaves, lay them on a piece of foam rubber and score the centre of each leaf with a wooden pick to form a vein. At the same time this will make the leaves curl up at the sides. Make clusters of berries from small balls of red marzipan.

ASSORTED SHAPES

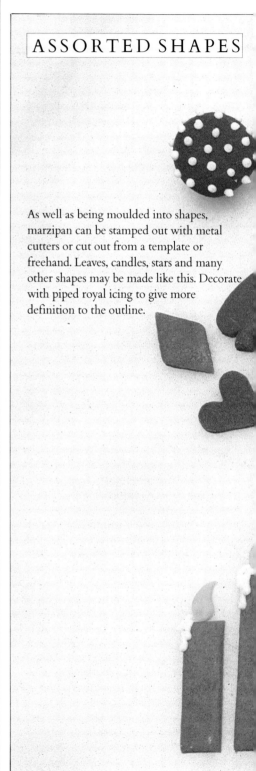

As well as being moulded into shapes, marzipan can be stamped out with metal cutters or cut out from a template or freehand. Leaves, candles, stars and many other shapes may be made like this. Decorate with piped royal icing to give more definition to the outline.

MARZIPAN MARQUETRY

This is a very effective way to decorate a cake and though it looks very elaborate, it is quite simple to produce. It is based on the ideas of marquetry and mosaics used in furniture and tile design.

Small pieces of different coloured marzipan are arranged in an interlocking pattern to cover the top of a cake. Any design you like can be used and it is a good idea to draw it first. Cut a piece of paper the exact size of the top of the cake, then draw the design on it, deciding how many colours you are going to use and marking the shapes with the appropriate colour. Make a copy of the finished design on greaseproof or waxed paper and cut it into the individual pieces. Arrange these on the original pattern until you are ready to cut out the pieces.

Colour the marzipan by simply kneading a little edible food colouring into each piece. Have some apricot glaze ready to attach the pieces to the cake.

The sides of the cake should be decorated first; this can be done with one continuous strip of almond paste, or two half strips. Follow the method for covering a cake with almond paste on page 69, or cover with butter cream and a coating such as praline.

Roll out one piece of coloured marzipan on a surface lightly dusted with icing sugar or cornflour and cut out all the pieces in that colour. Repeat with the other colours, then build up the pattern on the cake, attaching each piece with a little apricot glaze and ensuring that all the pieces interlock neatly.

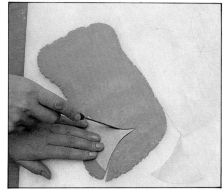

1 Place each template on the appropriately coloured marzipan and cut around it.

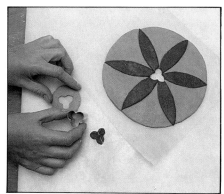

2 Assemble the pieces on greaseproof paper to check that they fit together neatly.

3 Transfer to the top of the cake, one by one, attaching the pieces with apricot glaze.

PAINTING WITH FOOD COLOUR

There is a great variety of food colouring and cake decorating materials available on the market today, making it possible to achieve a wide range of decorative effects. The range of colours is constantly being extended, and the quality of colours improving. The most common method of colouring icing is to add it to the icing, and then apply the icing to the cake. Unfortunately, there are certain circumstances where this produces rather false colours. Leaf green, for example, when added to icing, never produces an authentic leaf colour, no matter how much colour is used. However, leaf green does produce a beautiful and authentic shade of green if the food colour is used as a paint. In fact, by using the colour in this way it is possible not only to reproduce more subtle and true life shades, but also to achieve a greater variety of decorative effects.

1 Food colours can be used like any watercolour paint. For example, adding water will make the colour paler and mixing different colours can produce some interesting and exciting shades of colour.

2 In order to make food colours fade into each other, apply the chosen colours to the surface being decorated so that they lie immediately next to each other. Whilst the colours are still wet, make gentle brushstrokes across where the colours meet, merging one into the other.

3 To produce wood grain effect, mix the colour required in a palette or saucer. Using a medium-sized paintbrush, dip the brush into the colour shaking off any excess colouring. The brush should not be too wet. Press the brush down on to a work surface so that the bristles splay out into points. Gently brush across the surface of the icing to produce several lines.

RIGHT: *Food colour comes in several different forms: as powder, paste, liquid and fibre-tip pens. Experiment with the different types until you find the one that suits you best. A couple of fine paintbrushes and a white saucer or an artist's plastic palette are the only other materials you will need.*

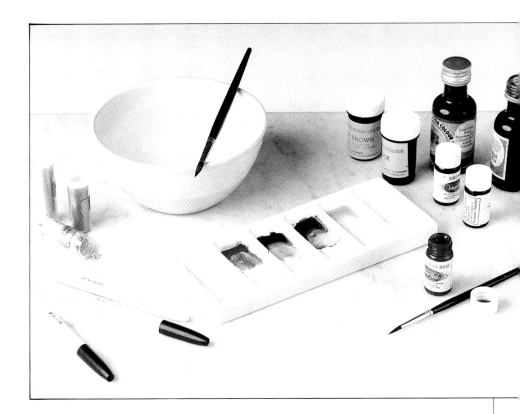

If you are painting two different colours directly beside each other or one colour over the top of another as LEFT, let the first colour dry completely before applying the second. Otherwise the colours will bleed into each other.

4 To produce a colour wash effect, make sure that the brush is full of colour. If you have to dip the brush too often, you risk creating a streaked effect. Gently brush backwards and forwards until the surface is completely covered. Let the colours dry. Once dry it is possible to paint a design over the wash without disturbing the colour background, as illustrated.

5 When painting certain details or designs on a cake, it might be helpful to have an outline drawn on the cake beforehand using either black food colour or a food colour pen. In either case be sure to let the outline dry completely before filling in the colours, as illustrated.

6 To produce a stippled or marbled effect, mix the colours required and make sure the brush is not too wet. Press the brush down vertically on to a counter so that the bristles splay out into a rough circle of points. Lift the brush and holding it vertically, lightly dot the surface of the icing, as illustrated. In all cases when colour decorating, *practise* on a spare piece of icing before painting the design on to the cake.

Chapter Four:
ADVANCED ICING TECHNIQUES

A useful way of practising the techniques in the chapter is to ice a polystyrene cake dummy and then try out the different piping techniques on it. This will help you choose your cake design, by giving you a chance to discover which types of decoration you like and find easy.

This section opens with the fundamentals — basic equipment and icing tips. It then demonstrates a variety of piping techniques, making lace, run-outs, piping flowers and borders and finally making templates for positioning pillars on tiered cakes and assembling tiers.

Equipment

The equipment illustrated opposite is a selection of items used in the decoration of elaborate royal- and fondant-iced celebration cakes.

1 Heavy-duty icing turntable
2 Plaster wedding cakes pillars
3 Plastic wedding cake pillars, with hollow centres for wooden skewers
4 Polystyrene cake dummy for practice and display purposes
5 Wooden skewers
6 A selection of shaped 1cm/½in cake boards and thin cake cards
7 Large flexible plastic icing smoother or plain icing comb for fondant icing
8 Small stainless steel scraper for royal icing
9 Small flexible plastic smoother or plain icing comb
10 Stainless steel straight edge for applying royal icing
11 Short spatula for general mixing and filling work
12 Handled smoother or icing comb for fondant icing an alternative to the large flexible smoother
13 Silver banding for cakes and cake boards

ICING TIPS

There are many different kinds of icing tips on the market. It is better to buy the more expensive tips because they have very finely cut edges, which give accurate shapes and are more durable. If you buy inexpensive tips and find that the edges are rather rough or banned, file them down with emery paper.

All the shapes — star, shell, petal, basket weave, leaf and so on — come in varying widths. A full range comprises between 15 and 25 sizes.

To begin with, you will need a fine writing tip, which is round and also produces a beaded 'snail trail', a shell tip and perhaps a petal tip. With these three basic tools you can create a wide range of designs.

Icing tips should always be kept clean —

even a fine obstruction, such as a hair, can spoil the regular outline of the shape you are trying to pipe. A special icing tip brush is available for cleaning tips.

Different manufacturers use different numbers to designate the widths of the tips, but smaller numbers in this always refer to finer tips. The tips used in this book are made by Bekenal Products Ltd. (For Wilton tip equivalents, see page 133.)

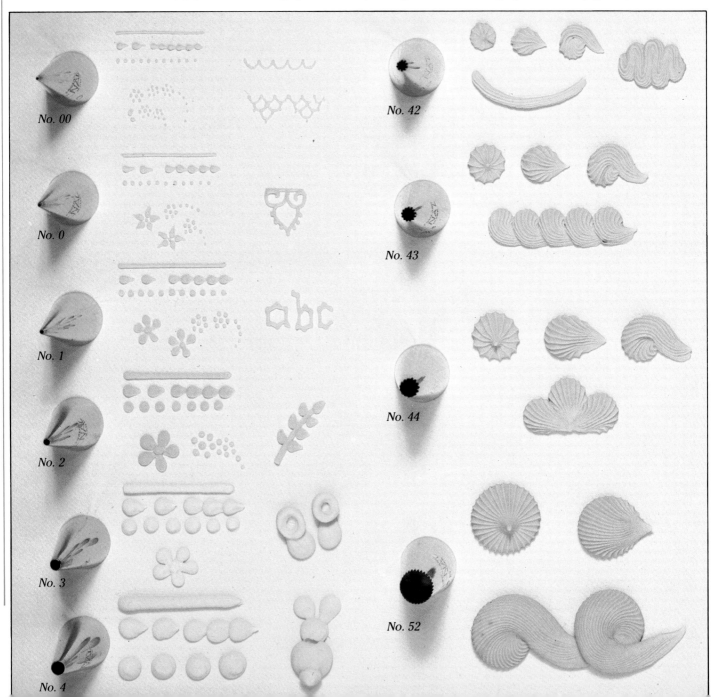

No. 00

No. 0

No. 1

No. 2

No. 3

No. 4

No. 42

No. 43

No. 44

No. 52

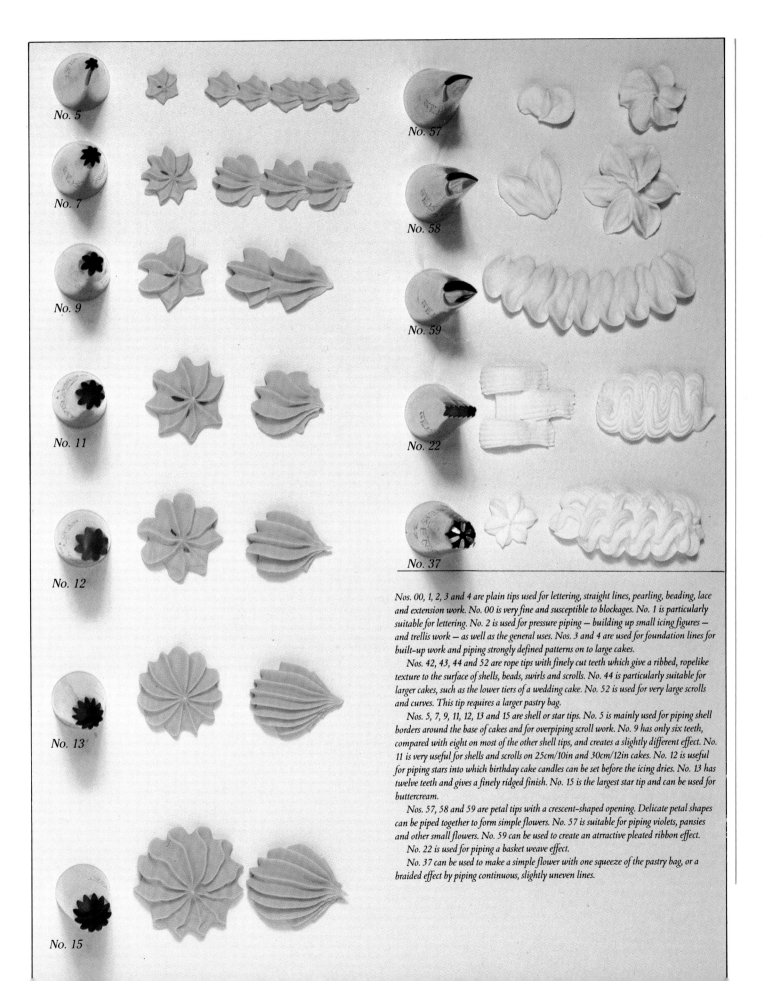

Nos. 00, 1, 2, 3 and 4 are plain tips used for lettering, straight lines, pearling, beading, lace and extension work. No. 00 is very fine and susceptible to blockages. No. 1 is particularly suitable for lettering. No. 2 is used for pressure piping — building up small icing figures — and trellis work — as well as the general uses. Nos. 3 and 4 are used for foundation lines for built-up work and piping strongly defined patterns on to large cakes.

Nos. 42, 43, 44 and 52 are rope tips with finely cut teeth which give a ribbed, ropelike texture to the surface of shells, beads, swirls and scrolls. No. 44 is particularly suitable for larger cakes, such as the lower tiers of a wedding cake. No. 52 is used for very large scrolls and curves. This tip requires a larger pastry bag.

Nos. 5, 7, 9, 11, 12, 13 and 15 are shell or star tips. No. 5 is mainly used for piping shell borders around the base of cakes and for overpiping scroll work. No. 9 has only six teeth, compared with eight on most of the other shell tips, and creates a slightly different effect. No. 11 is very useful for shells and scrolls on 25cm/10in and 30cm/12in cakes. No. 12 is useful for piping stars into which birthday cake candles can be set before the icing dries. No. 13 has twelve teeth and gives a finely ridged finish. No. 15 is the largest star tip and can be used for buttercream.

Nos. 57, 58 and 59 are petal tips with a crescent-shaped opening. Delicate petal shapes can be piped together to form simple flowers. No. 57 is suitable for piping violets, pansies and other small flowers. No. 59 can be used to create an attractive pleated ribbon effect.

No. 22 is used for piping a basket weave effect.

No. 37 can be used to make a simple flower with one squeeze of the pastry bag, or a braided effect by piping continuous, slightly uneven lines.

MAKING ROYAL ICING

Working with royal icing is the single most important aspect of cake decorating. It is used both for piping and for covering the cake.

Royal icing, or glacé royale, as it is also known, is made by beating together sugar and egg whites. The action of beating incorporates millions of minute air bubbles into the mixture, and it is this that gives it its texture. Well made royal icing can be easily cut with a sharp knife.

The slightest trace of egg yolk or grease, however, will break down the egg white and prevent it from becoming properly aerated, no matter how much you beat it. One solution is to keep the bowl and other equipment you use for making royal icing for that purpose alone. Alternatively, you can make sure your bowl is greasefree by washing it out with hot, soapy water, rinsing it under hot water and then standing it upside down to drain. Let it dry off by itself. If you need to dry it quickly, use a freshly laundered tea towel.

Never beat royal icing in a plastic bowl, because you may scrape tiny slivers of plastic of it as you beat. If you transfer the icing to a plastic bowl in order to store it, again make sure the bowl is completely grease-free.

MAKING ROYAL ICING BY HAND

Royal icing made by hand often has a better consistency than that made in a mixer, because you can judge by the feel of it when to add more sugar and when the icing is ready.

Ingredients

1 egg white, room temperature
about 2½ cups powdered sugar, sifted
twice just before using
strained juice of half a lemon

If the icing is to be used for coating the cake only, weigh out the correct amount and put it in a clean bowl, then add 1 tsp glycerine per 1½ cups. This will help to give an icing that will cut without splintering.

1 Break up the egg white with a metal spatula making sure that both the spatula and the bowl are free from grease. A metal spatula cuts and aerates the white more effectively than a metal spoon.

2 Very gradually add the finely sifted sugar, working each addition in well with the metal spatula before adding the next. Only add half a tablespoon at a time. If you add it too quickly and do not beat it enough in between additions, the result will be too much sugar in the icing, and this will give it a dull yellowish colour. Stir frequently round the sides of the bowl to incorporate the sugar sticking to it, and every time you do so, scrape off the knife on the edge of the bowl to stop sugar building up on the blade.

ROYAL ICING INGREDIENTS

Egg white
It is a good idea to break and separate the eggs you are going to use for royal icing two or three hours before making it, or even the night before. This will allow some of the water to evaporate from the white, which increases its viscosity and makes a stronger icing.

Reconstituted albumen powder can be substituted for fresh egg white in royal icing. Use it according to the manufacturer's instructions.

Separate the egg white or albumen mixture into a grease free bowl and cover it with a dampened cloth to prevent it completely drying out.

Sugar
The amount of powdered sugar you need is impossible to specify exactly, because it depends on the quantity of egg white. Sift the sugar twice through a fine sieve, or it may block decorating tips and cause you a great deal of frustrations.

Additives
Some people add a little acetic acid or cream of tartar to royal icing to increase its frothing power and to strengthen it. Be careful not to add too much, or it will give the sugar a strong pungent odour, spoil the colour and harden the icing. Adding a squeeze of lemon juice both whitens the icing and gives it more elasticity. This is useful while you are working with the icing, but once it has set, the lemon juice tends to make it more brittle and liable to crack when you cut the cake. Therefore, only add lemon juice to icing which is to be used for piping, but not for covering the cake.

If you use an additive in the covering icing, be sure to use exactly the same amount if you make a second batch of icing, otherwise the result will be patchy.

If you find the icing very hard and splintery when you cut the cake, it is because not enough air has been incorporated into it by beating. Some cake decorators add 1 tsp glycerine per 3⅓ cups powdered sugar. This will make the icing a little softer. Only add glycerine to icing for covering the cake, not for piping.

3 As you add your sugar, the syrup thickens until you can pull it into a peak when you lift the knife out of it. Once the icing is stiff enough to hold a peak, add a squeeze of lemon juice. If this wets the icing too much, incorporate a little more sugar. The lemon juice will give the icing a smoother, creamier feel. Remember that a firmer consistency is needed for piping borders and a softer consistency for line work.

4 To store the icing, you must protect it from moisture. Carefully wipe off the sides of the bowl with a clean cloth to remove every particle of sugar.

5 Take a piece of plastic wrap and press it right down on to the icing, smoothing it to eliminate any air bubbles. Put another layer of plastic wrap across the top of the bowl and seal the bowl in an airtight container. You can store it in this way for up to two weeks. Do not put the icing in the refrigerator because it will absorb moisture, and this spoils its consistency.

MAKING ROYAL ICING IN A MIXER

You can also make royal icing in a mixer. It will save you a lot of hard work, but you will not be able to judge the consistency with the same accuracy. Always keep the beater on the lowest speed — if you beat it fast you will incorporate too much air into it and large bubbles may appear as you ice the cake.

The basic principle is the same as for making the icing by hand. The following photographs show the technique using dried egg powder — pure albumen — egg substitute, or a boosted albumen.

Ingredients

675g/1½lb 3⅓ cups sugar, sifted twice
75ml/3fl oz/⅓ cup water
1½tbsp or 7tsp albumen powder

1 First mix the water and albumen into a small bowl. The resulting liquid will be sloppy and lumpy and give off a strong smell. Do not give up and throw it away! Albumen does have a strong smell. It has a very long shelf life and the smell does not mean it has gone bad. Do not try to whip out the lumps of coagulated albumen. Let it stand for at least 15 minutes, or a couple of hours, or overnight if possible, to dissolve.

2 Sieve the albumen and water mixture into the mixing bowl. Add half the sugar and beat it until you have a smooth consistency, remembering to wipe down the sides of the bowl frequently to incorporate any sugar that may be sticking to it. Then add the rest of the sugar and, if you are using pure albumen, beat it for 12–14 minutes. If you are using boosted albumen, you should reach the right consistency after beating for only about 4 minutes. Boosted albumen contains a foaming agent that helps it reach the right consistency much quicker than normal egg white, and therefore it needs less beating. If you overbeat it, your icing will be be very hard and splintery.

3 When the right consistency is reached, when it can stand up in soft peaks, seal and store the icing as for handmade icing.

USING ROYAL ICING

Quantities of royal icing required to give two coats to top and sides of a fruit cake

The g/lb quantity refers to the weight of icing sugar required.

Size of cake	Quantity of royal icing
15cm/6in square 18cm/7in round	550g/1¼lb
18cm/7in square 20cm/8in round	675g/1½lb
20cm/8in square 23cm/9in round	900g/2lb
23cm/9in square 25cm/10in round	1kg/2¼lb
25cm/10in square 28cm/11in round	1.2kb/2½lb
28cm/11in square 30cm/12in round	1.4kg/3lb
30cm/12in square	1.6kg/3½lb

Rough or peaked icing

This gives a quick finish to cakes where time is short. It is generally used on Christmas cakes to give an 'icicle effect' to the sides of the cake, or a general 'snow covering'. The same principle may be followed using frostings. Add sufficient icing sugar so that the icing will stand in stiff peaks if pulled up with the back of a wooden spoon.

Spread icing evenly over the top and sides of the cake (already covered with marzipan). Using the tip of a round-ended knife, or a palette knife, pull up the icing at regular intervals to form peaks. Leave to set for about 8 hours.

Extra decorations, such as marzipan shapes or bought decorations should be placed in position before the icing dries.

COLOURING ROYAL ICING

It is difficult to achieve strong royal icing colours, such as Christmas red, royal blue, moss green or black, with the standard food colours widely available in general stores. Better colours are achieved with food colours designed for the purpose, available from specialist sources.

Food colours come in several forms — as liquid, powder, syrup or paste. Powder is not recommended as it is extremely messy to use. Both paste and liquid colours maintain the consistency of the royal icing, and are the most suitable.

In order to achieve a bright red or true black, it is important to allow the colour to 'wet out' in the icing — that is, to let the icing stand for 20-30 minutes while the colour strength develops.

Flat icing

An even flat surface is essential on a cake that is to be piped and decorated. It is a fairly lengthy process and requires much patience and perseverance! Cakes should have a minimum of two coats of icing, but three coats give a really professional finish. The top and sides of the cake have to be iced on separate days, so that one surface is not spoiled while neatening the other. One day between each coat of icing is sufficient, so allow at least 4 days for flat icing, and this should be started about 10-14 days before the cake is required.

To flat ice the top of a cake

Place the cake (already covered with marzipan) on a board and secure with a generous dab of icing. Place the board on a non-slip work surface.

1 Spoon some icing on the top of the cake. Spread the icing over the top of the cake with a palette knife using a 'paddling' movement. This works out any air bubbles.

2 Using an icing rule held at an angle of about 45 degrees, draw the edge towards you over the surface of the icing in one smooth, continuous movement, taking care to press evenly but not too heavily. If the resulting surface is not sufficiently smooth, spoon a little more icing on to the cake and repeat the complete process (using a clean ruler).

3 Smooth off the edges of the icing by running a palette knife or plain-edged icing ruler round the top of the cake. Leave to dry.

To flat ice the sides of a cake

It is preferable to place the cake on a turntable at this stage, but if you haven't got one it is possible to improvize with a large plate over an upturned mixing bowl.

For a round cake: Spread an even layer of icing all over the sides of the cake using the same paddling movement as mentioned above.

Holding a plain-edged icing comb in one hand at an angle of about 45 degrees to the surface of the cake, and using the other hand to move the turntable slowly and evenly, start at the back of the cake and draw the comb around the icing to give a smooth finish. In effect, the icing comb is held in the same position while the free hand rotates the turntable through a full circle.

Scrape off any excess icing from the top edge and the board with a palette knife or icing comb. Leave to dry. Once dry, clean the board with a damp cloth.

For a square cake: The same basic principles apply, but there are four corners to consider, which must be kept as neat and even as possible. Beginners may find it easier to do a square cake in two stages, icing opposite sides on one day, then icing the remaining two opposite sides on the next day. If so, do allow plenty of time for this.

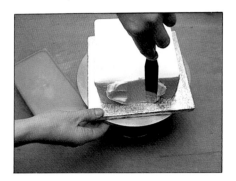

Icing the sides

1 Spread the icing over two sides of the cake, then draw the icing comb over the surface to give a neat finish.

Using a palette knife, cut off the icing at both corners to give a neat straight edge. Trim off any excess icing and leave to dry.

Repeat the same process with the remaining two sides.

2 When the icing is dry, check to see how even it is. If necessary, use a clean piece of fine sandpaper to rub off any small bumps and level the surface. Remove the icing dust with a clean pastry brush.

For the second and third coats of icing, repeat the icing process once or twice more as wished, but ensure that each coat is dry before starting on the next. Leave to dry for at least 24 hours before adding any piped or moulded decorations.

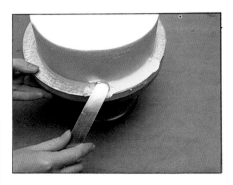

Icing the cake board

1 Although the cake board is often used as it is, it may be iced as well. To do this allow the iced cake to dry completely on the board, then spread a thin layer of icing over the board, smoothing it with a palette knife.

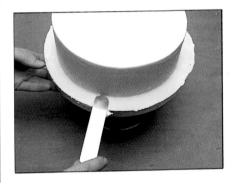

2 Using the same technique of rotating the turntable with one hand and holding the icing comb or palette knife in the other, smooth the icing by holding the icing comb at an angle to the board and just touching it. Neaten the edges and leave to dry.

Decorating with a serrated icing comb

1 A quick and attractive finish can be made using an icing comb with a serrated edge. Flat ice the sides of the cake and leave to dry.

2 For the second coat use a contrasting colour of icing, if wished. Coat the sides of the cake with the icing, then, instead of smoothing the surface, draw a serrated icing comb over the sides, either in a straight or curved movement. The final effect is that of contrasting stripes. Leave to dry.

PIPING DESIGNS AND DECORATIONS

Piping is not difficult as long as you take things slowly, start with the simplest piping design and master it before you attempt the next stage. The hardest aspect is finding the patience to keep practising! Royal icing is fairly cheap to make and lasts for weeks in an airtight container, so if you have a spare half-hour, practise on a work surface, or a baking sheet.

The consistency of royal icing is very important when piping. Make sure it is stiff enough to stand in soft peaks when pulled up with a spoon. If the peak becomes shiny almost as soon as you have pulled it up, the icing is a little too soft, so beat in a little extra sifted icing sugar. If it is too stiff it can be thinned down with a tiny amount of unbeaten egg white or water.

Piping designs

Most designs are made with a plain (writing) nozzle or a star nozzle. However, there are several nozzles that make specific designs, for example, shell, basket and petal.

Make sure the nozzle tip is clean and free from icing for a neat piped line.

Using a plain nozzle (Nos. 1, 2 or 3)

Straight lines: Squeeze out the icing until it just touches the cake. Squeeze gently allowing a slightly sagging line of icing to appear from the nozzle just above the surface of the cake, at the same time pulling the piping bag towards you. Stop squeezing the icing just before the end of the line and touch the surface of the cake to finish the line and break the icing neatly.

Loops or scallops: As for straight lines but following the line of a scallop (curved) design.

Trellis: This is a series of straight parallel lines crossed at right angles by another series of parallel lines. Always start in the centre and pipe lines to either side of this original line.

Writing: This may be done freehand but do practise first. Icing can easily be scraped off the iced surface if an error is made. It is perhaps a good idea to make a template of the words to be written and to prick them on to the surface of the cake with a pin.

Numbering: This can be done in the same way as writing. Stencils will give a more professional finish, but perhaps the most bold effect can be achieved with run-outs (pages 122-5).

Rope: This is achieved by piping in a circular movement in a clockwise direction, piping each loop overlapping the last. The loops may be even or decreasing towards the end of the movement; this makes a leaf design.

Dots: Simply squeeze out the icing to the required size of dot and pull the icing bag away. The points may be pressed down to give a rounded effect, or a silver ball may be pressed into each. Smaller dots of a different colour may be piped on top of the original dot.

Lace effect: Hold the nozzle close to the surface of the cake and pipe a continuous wiggly line.

Lace edging: Pipe freehand decorative patterns. If wished they can be left to dry, then attached to the cake, overhanging the edge.

PIPING TECHNIQUES

The consistency of the icing is the most important factor in piping. It should not be too stiff — it must be light and fluffy and it must hold a peak.

Stars

Stars can be piped with tips Nos. 5, 7, 9, 11, 12, 13 or 15. Hold the bag, fitted with the appropriate tip, perpendicular to the surface to be iced. Press on the bag to release the icing, then pull it up gently to form a paint and a star shape will be formed.

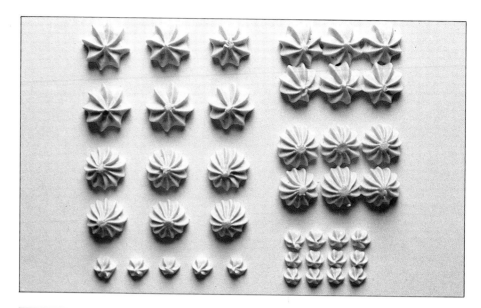

Rosettes

You can use Nos. 42, 43 and 44. These rosettes are made with fine rope tips, which have shallower indentations than the star tips. With the bag held perpendicular to the surface to be iced, pipe a circle. Lift the tip slightly, apply pressure, bring it round to the centre and release the pressure as you tail it off.

Scrolls

Pipe scrolls with fine rope tips, as for rosettes, but instead of tailing off into the circle, come out of it, creating a C-or an S-shape. For a C-shape, work in a counterclockwise motion. For an S-shape, take the tip round clockwise. You can make attractive patterns by combining the C and the S and, if you twist the tip as you pipe, you will get a rope effect.

Alternating shells

You can use tips Nos. 5 and 13. Follow the instructions for shells, but take the point down at an angle of 45 degrees. Pipe a second row of shells beneath the first, taking the points up. Start with your piping tip at the tail of the upper shell for a braided effect.

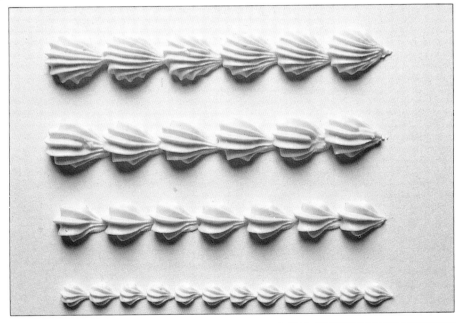

Shells

You can use tips Nos. 13, 11, 8 and 5. Rest the appropriate tip on the surface where you want to pipe the shell. Push out the icing without moving the bag. Once the shell has formed, pull the bag back to form a tail. Position the bag to form the next shell so that it just overlaps the tail of the one in front.

Fleur-de-lis

This shape can be piped with a shell tip No. 13 or fine rope tip Nos. 44, 43 or 42 or you can even use a plain round tip for a smooth effect. First pipe a shell with a long tail. Then pipe an S-shape scroll to the left and a C-shape scroll to the right. You can pipe the flowers in the same way. Pipe one set of petals and overpipe the second set.

Straight lines

You can use tips Nos. 4, 3, 2, 1 and 0. Touch the surface where you want to pipe. Lift the tip and apply pressure so that the icing flows out in a straight line. Drop it down at the other end of the line after you have released the pressure and the icing has stopped flowing. Do not attempt to pipe a straight line by dragging the tip along the surface of the cake or wax paper. All you will succeed in doing is damaging the fine edge of the tip and indenting the surface of the cake. The tip must be lifted off the surface.

Overpiping is a classic piping technique. It takes practice and requires a very steady hand. By piping straight lines of varying widths touching each other, you can create a classic three-dimensional effect. Let each line dry before you begin on the next. If you are using this technique on a wedding cake, complete all your piping with one width tip before you change to the next. If you make a mistake, you can correct it with a slightly damp paintbrush, by pushing the line back into shape.

Trellis

You will need tip No. 1. Pipe one set of parallel lines, then overpipe a second either at right angles for squares, or with both sets of lines on the diagonal for diamonds. Use another width tip for overpiping to create a different effect.

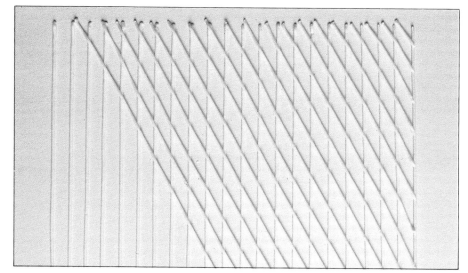

Zigzags

You can use tips Nos. 42, 5 or 3. These can be piped in a continuous line with any shaped tip. Until you are more confident, you may find it easier to stop and start at each point — this will give a very definite V-shape to the zigzag.

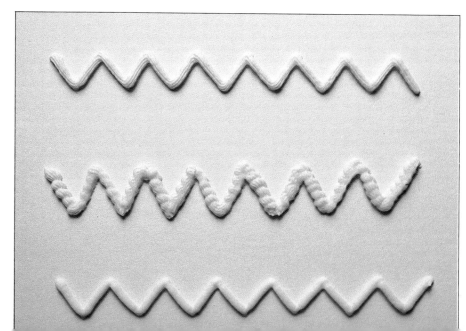

Raised trellis or nets

You can use tips Nos. 43, 3, 2 and 1. This is a style that was very popular a couple of decades ago. It has now gone out of fashion because it is time-consuming. You can build up from the base with trellis work, but it is quicker and just as effective to pipe an oval scroll with a fine rope tip and cover it. Anchor the icing, twist the tip to form a rope as you apply the pressure, then release the pressure and taper off. Overpipe with a fine round tip, making parallel diagonal lines. Overpipe again in the opposite direction. You can build up the net by overpiping with decreasing sized tips in different directions.

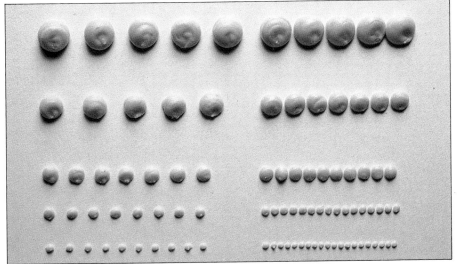

Dots and beads

You can use tips Nos. 4, 3, 2, 1 and 0. The difficulty with piping dots and beads is disguising the take-off point, which will tend to make a tail. This is harder to disguise, the bigger the bead you are piping. Using constant pressure keep the point of the tip stationary in the bead until it is the size required. Release pressure on the bag after piping the bead and then take off gently to the side. Correct any mistakes with a slightly dampened brush once the bead is nearly dry by gently pressing any projecting point down into the mass of icing. The larger beads are almost always overpiped.

Twisted rope

You can use tips Nos. 44, 43, 42 and 5. Twisted rope can be piped with a plain writing tip or a shell tip as well as a rope tip. The trick is to twist the bag as you are piping. Keep constant pressure on the bag. To avoid varying the width of the rope, hold the bag at an angle and rotate it as you go.

Cornelli

You will need nozzle tip No. 1. Cornelli or scribbling is an attractive texturing technique achieved by piping a maze of W-shapes and M-shapes in a continuous line but at random over a confined space. Use a fine tip and avoid moving in straight lines – you should not be able to see where the work begins or ends.

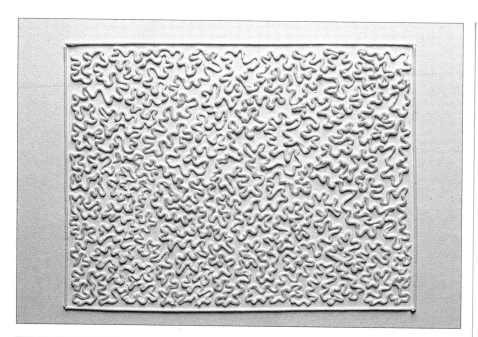

Embroidery

Embroidery work makes a very attractive decoration for the side of a cake. The illustration shows a complete pattern and then the elements that make it up. Use tip No. 0 or 1 and pipe a row of blue built-up circles 2.5cm/1in apart. Pipe two similar circles above the first, two below the second and so on alternating throughout the pattern. This is a reliable method of achieving an even pattern. Pipe a forget-me-not between each group of built-up circles. Finally add the leaves with green royal icing.

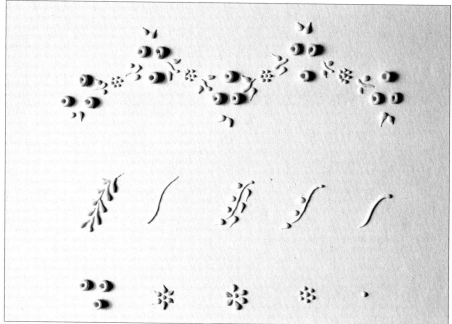

Making lace

Lace is always the last decoration to be added to a cake because it is so fragile and breaks so easily. Take great care when handling lace or when moving a cake with lace attached.

Designs for lacework are simple and varied. Patterns with several joints are stronger than those where the lines cross in only one or two places.

Lace is piped separately on to wax paper, left to dry, then carefully lifted off and attached to the cake with fine lines of royal icing.

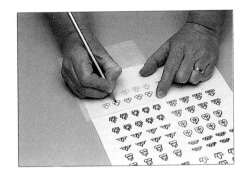

1 Choose a pattern and copy it 40 to 80 times on to a 15cm/6in square piece of tracing paper, depending on the size of the lace. Use a sharp pencil or fine fibre tip pen. Each piece of lace is 1cm/½in wide, so it is easy to work out how much you will need. Six sheets with 40 to 80 pieces of lace will be enough for a three-tiered wedding cake. It is a good idea, however, to pipe half as many pieces again as you will actually need if you are a beginner, because you are likely to break several pieces.

2 Tape the four corners of the tracing paper securely to a work surface. Tape a larger piece of wax paper over the pattern with masking tape. Only use a couple of pieces so that you do not disturb the piped lace too much when you remove the tape.

3 With tip No. 0 or 1, pipe the lace in any direction that feels comfortable. Ensure that each piece of lace has a flat bar where it is to be attached to the cake. Wipe the end of the tip with your fingers or a damp cloth between each piece of lace to ensure clean lines. For particularly elaborate lace, use different coloured icing for different sections of each piece. The bar should be the same colour as the icing on the cake.

4 If you make a mistake, it can be corrected with a fine paintbrush. The paintbrush should be slightly dampened, but not wet.

5 Let the lace dry for at least two hours or overnight if possible. Do not put the lace in the oven to dry as the wax paper will melt into the icing.

6 To remove the lace, curl the wax paper over the index finger of your left hand. The lace will begin to release. Slide a metal spatula under the piece of lace and gently lift it off. Never try to remove lace with tweezers, as the slightest pressure will break the lace. The lace is now ready to attach to the cake.

Basket weaving

This is actually quite easy to do and gives a very professional finish to a cake. You will need two icing nozzles — a basket or ribbon nozzle and a plain nozzle (No. 2 or No. 3).

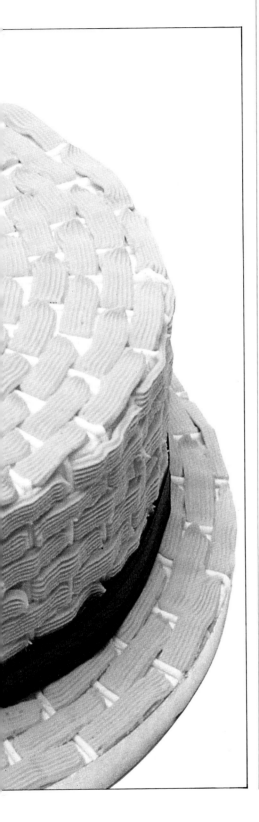

1 Give the cake a basic flat coat of royal icing. It does not matter if this is slightly uneven as it will be totally covered by the basket work.

2 With an icing bag fitted with the plain nozzle, pipe a series of vertical parallel lines around the cake at regular intervals. Leave to dry.

3 With a second icing bag fitted with the basket or ribbon nozzle, start the horizontal weaving at the base of the cake. Hold the nozzle at the side of one vertical line and squeeze out a ribbon of icing. Lift it over the second vertical line and finish at the side of the third vertical line. Start the next strip at the other side of the third vertical line. Repeat this all the way round the base of the cake.

4 Start the next row of weaving, but make sure you begin the piping at the second vertical line. Continue around the cake, building up the woven appearance.

MAKING MOULDS AND SHAPES IN TRELLIS AND LACE WORK

This takes quite a bit of practice, but some very pretty decorations and effects can be achieved. Start with simple shapes, such as small tartlet tins, patty tins and boat-shaped moulds. Special icing moulds are available as well.

1 Other shapes, such as baskets, can be built up by piping shapes on to non– stick paper.

2 Fill these in with trellis or lace work and once dry, secure the pieces together with a little icing.

1 Lightly grease the mould with oil.

2 Using a No. 2 icing nozzle, pipe trellis or lace work over the surface of the mould starting at one edge.

3 Slowly move along the mould until the other end is reached.

4 Finally cover the bottom.

5 Strengthen the trellis with several vertical lines piped around the outside.

6 Leave for at least 24 hours to dry, then carefully remove from the mould.

RUN-OUTS

This technique involves piping an outline and flooding it, giving a good flat shape with cleanly rounded edges. It is also called flooding or running. The run-outs are usually piped on wax paper, left to dry then lifted off and used to decorate the cake. However, in some cases it is simpler to pipe run-out designs directly on to the cake, especially if the design is a figure or fairly complicated shape.

Icing for run-outs

When you make up royal icing for run-outs, it should be to normal piping consistency. It should not be too moist or the icing will not set quickly and will be too weak. Make it in the normal way, then thin it down a little with beaten egg white or water. If you use egg white, the icing will be stronger, but it may take up to a week to dry. It is better to use water and add it, literally, a drop at a time. Use an eye dropper to get the consistency exactly right. Do not beat the icing as you are adding the water because you will incorporate too much air. Just stir it gently.

Add enough water so that your icing is of a piping consistency. To judge the amount of water to add, swirl a knife in the bowl and count steadily to 10 as the ripples subside. The icing should just have found its own level as you get to 10 (about 5 seconds).

Icing collars, filigree pieces and designs that are subsequently lifted before placing in position are always piped on to wax paper,

over an outline. The outline obviously acts as a guide, but its other purpose is to stop the flooded icing from contracting as it dries — not to stop it spreading. It will only spread if your icing is too runny.

It is important to dry run-outs as quickly as possible in order to get a good sheen or surface finish. A warm cupboard is often a good place.

Piping a run-out

1 The first step in making a run-out is to secure a piece of wax paper to a counter over the outline you want to fill in. Attach a tag to the paper on which the outline is drawn, so you can easily slide it out from the wax paper afterwards. Do not use parchment paper as a substitute for wax, as it may wrinkle. Draw the outline with a dark coloured fibre tip or a sharp pencil. Put the paper was side up to facilitate the release of the run-out when it dries. Use masking tape, which pulls off more easily than conventional scotch tape, to secure it. Wrenching away a piece of adhesive tape may break your run-out. Do not tape right around the wax paper — you may trap air underneath and the damp icing on top will cause the paper to lift and buckle the run-out as it dries. Secure the paper only at the corners.

2 If you are piping a collar, or anything with a middle hollow, make a small cut in the shape of a cross in the centre of the paper to relax the natural tension in the fabric of the paper.

3 Pipe the outline carefully following the line of the pattern on the tracing beneath.

4 Fill a pastry bag with flooding icing, but do not cut the hole in the bottom until you are ready to make the run-out, or the icing will pour straight out of it. Make sure that the hole you cut is not too big or you might lose control. A tip is not necessary for flooding.

5 Start close to your outline, but do not touch it with the bag, or you may break it. Keeping the tip of the bag in the icing to reduce the chance of air bubbles forming, allow the icing to flow out, moving the bag backwards and forwards across the shape as you do so.

6 When you have almost filled the whole area, use a paintbrush to push the icing right out to the edge of the line, so that it just spills on to it. This way you get a good smooth edge.

7 Make sure there are no air bubbles in the icing by gently tapping the board on the work surface. When any appear, smooth them away with your brush.

8 Remove the pattern from beneath the paper by the tag. If you are making a whole series of run-outs, you can use the same pattern each time. Let the run-outs dry.

Butterflies

First pipe the inside of the wings with cornelli or other fine piping work. Then pipe the outline of the wings and flood first the bottom part and then the top.

When the wings are dry, pipe teardrop-shaped piece of icing for the body. Attach the wings to it while it is still wet and support them with cotton balls until they have set in position. Use stamens for antennae, but remember that they are not edible.

9 Once a run-out is dry, you can remove it from the paper by working a cranked metal spatula (one with a thin angled blade) underneath it all the way round or by peeling the paper off the back, taking care not to break the run-out. With a large collar, the easiest way to peel off the backing is to pull it down, away from the run-out over the edge of the counter. Work half way round until the run-out is nearly free. Then turn it through 180 degrees and peel off the other side.

Monograms and numbers

The important thing to decide here is which part of the design should be the most prominent. Pipe the back of the design first.

In the monogram 'NC', the visible parts of the C are piped first, because the N lies on top of it.

In the number 8, the crossover bar is slightly raised, so this should be piped last. Do not try and do it all at once, or it will merge into a completely flat shape.

Swans

These swans are double-flooded, that is, flooded on the front and back so they can be viewed from both sides. Their wings are piped and then the birds are piped and then the birds are assembled on a flooded base.

1 First pipe the outline on wax paper. Work on the rear bird first. Once the icing has lost its wet look and is dry enough to hold the line, flood the body of the rear swan and the head of the front swan.

2 Once the flooded icing has set, flood the body of the front swan. When the front swan has set, flood the head of the back swan, so that it lies over the head of the front swan and their necks are entwined.

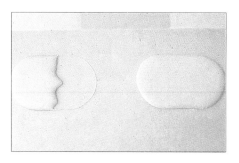

3 Pipe an outline for the base and flood it. Remember to keep the end of the tip in the icing. Take the icing right up to the piping line and brush it on to, but not right over the line.

4 Pipe the wings with a No. 3 tip, which is one of the larger round tips. Start at the base of the wing and pipe right up to the wing tip. Continue the line down to the base and back out to the wing tip again. Go back down beside this second line, and up to the tip again. This time continue the piping down to the centre of the wing and back out to the edge, to give the effect of feathers. Continue doing this until you get to the base of the wing. Each feather should be just touching the one beside it. Increase the pressure on the pastry bag at the tips of the feathers. When you reach the base make a swirl to give strength to the wing at the point where it will be attached to the body. Pipe all four wings in the same way.

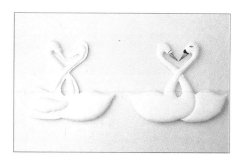

5 Once the swans are completely dry, lift them off the wax paper with a cranked metal spatula and turn them over. Pipe a little icing into the centres of the bodies and up the neck to stop them sagging when they dry. Flood the back of the swans in the same order that you flooded the front (see Steps 1 and 2). Let the swans dry completely before painting the beak and eyes with orange and black food colour on both sides.

6 To assemble the swans, pipe a line of royal icing, using tip No. 3 or No. 5, along the length of the base and set the swans down on to it.

7 Pipe a dab of icing on each side of each swan and attach wings. Support them until they are dry with cotton balls.

8 Choose ribbons and flowers for dressing the swans in colours to match your cake. Make ribbon loops and assemble the flower sprays and pieces of tulle caught into bunches with twisted wire.

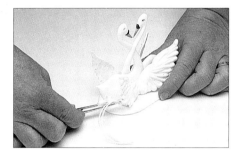

9 With your tweezers, carefully put a small piece of slightly dampened fondant icing behind the swan's wing. Be careful not to over-dampen the fondant icing or it will melt the royal icing.

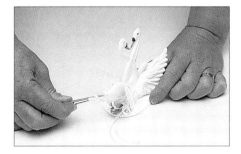

10 With the tweezers, carefully press the ribbon loops, flower sprays and tulle into the fondant ball. As the fondant dries, it will secure them.

Bells

Pipe the insides of the bells first and let them dry. Then pipe the top of the underneath bell. When that has dried, pipe the uppermost bell.

Rose

Start from the back of the design and work forwards, building it up in layers. As each step dries, fill in the next. Then finally fill in the centre petals.

Flower

For the maple leaf, work on opposite sides of the flower, which will not touch each other, before flooding the inside petals. When all five petals are dry, pipe in the centre.

Leaves

For holly and rose leaves, pipe the outline, flood half the leaf and let it dry, then flood the other half. The maple leaf is piped in four parts, letting each dry separately, to give a veined effect.

Shield and oval

These are simple designs, popular on cakes for club occasions. Pipe the outline, then flood in the centre. To give the shield a frame the flooding goes upwards, but not over the outline.

MAKING AND USING TEMPLATES

Most designs on formally iced cakes are geometric and so must be carefully measured and worked out as any unevenness will show up dramatically in the finished cake. The best way to ensure this is to draw the design first use this drawing or design as a guide to mark out the pattern on the cake. This design is known as a template.

Ideas for designs may come from lace or other materials, wallpaper or birthday and Christmas cards. Try a simple design at first, then progress to more elaborate ones as your piping expertise improves.

To make a template

Cut a piece of paper the exact size of the top of the cake. Fold the paper into sections, either four, six or eight. Mark a design on the top section, then cut along the line with scissors. Open out the paper to see the full effect of the design.

It is a good idea to copy the design on to

some thin card. The design can then be transferred to the cake by centering the template on the top of the cake and using a fine skewer or pin to prick or score the outline of the template. Pipe along the lines of the pattern, ensuring the icing covers the pin pricks or score marks. Any further icing which is added to build up the design can be done freehand once the basic pattern is piped.

Templates for the sides of cakes can also be made in a similar way. Measure the circumference of the cake and cut a piece of greaseproof or waxed paper to exactly the

same length and depth of the cake. Fold into sections to correspond with the template for the top of the cake. Draw the required design, then cut away the appropriate piece. Open out the paper to see the full design. Secure the paper in position arond the cake and mark out the design with a series of pin pricks or score it with a fine skewer.

The most popular design for the side of a cake is the scallop or hanging loop. With practice you will be able to do this freehand but it is a good idea to use a template for the

first attempts. You may also find it easier to tilt the cake slightly.

To pipe the loop, squeeze out a little icing and secure it in position at the start of the loop of the top edge of the cake. Squeeze out more icing so that it hangs in mid-air away from the cake. Once there is a sufficient length of icing, loop it up and attach it at the end of the first scallop marking. Continue around the cake in the same way. Follow the original lines to add furether icing. The icing does scrape off easily without leaving a mark, so don't worry too much about mistakes. As ever it is a good idea to practice on the side of a tin before you start the actual decorating.

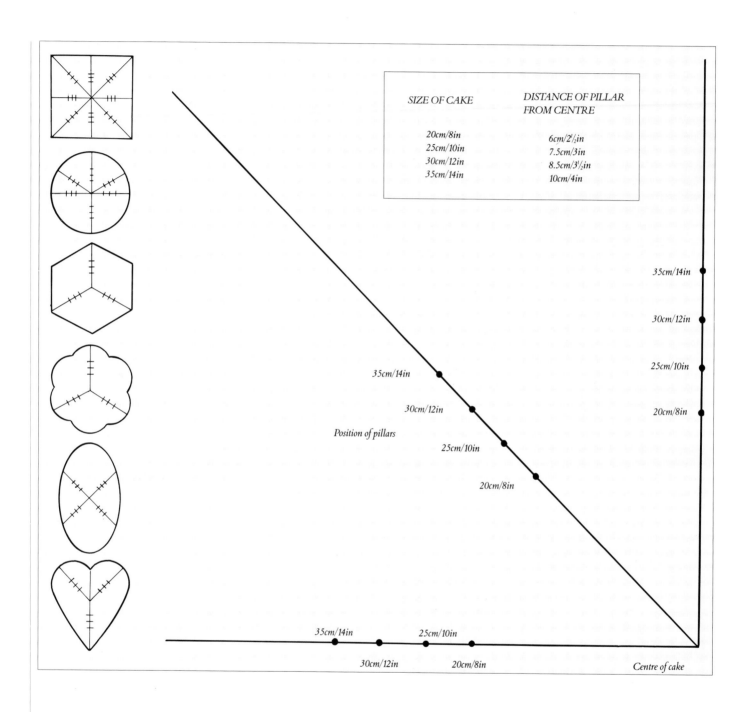

SIZE OF CAKE	DISTANCE OF PILLAR FROM CENTRE
20cm/8in	6cm/2½in
25cm/10in	7.5cm/3in
30cm/12in	8.5cm/3½in
35cm/14in	10cm/4in

Position of pillars

Centre of cake

The diagram ABOVE applies to all shapes of cake.
The points indicate how far each pillar should be positioned
from the centre of the cake for 4 sizes of cake, for example on
a 20cm/8in cake, each pillar should be 6cm/2½in from the
centre of the cake. This position will ensure maximum
stability for the supported tier.

TEMPLATES FOR POSITIONING PILLARS

The overall effect of an elaborately tiered cake can easily be spoiled by incorrectly positioned supporting pillars. The diagrams in this section show you how to work out where to position pillars on different-shaped cakes. The principles involved for most of the shapes are the same.

Templates can be made from paper or thin card. To obtain a good shape in each case, either draw round the cake pan and cut the shape out just inside the line to allow for the thickness of the pan or make a paper pattern following the instructions for each shape. You will need to make one template the size of the bottom tier for a two-tiered cake and two templates the size of the bottom and middle tiers for a three-tiered cake.

For some shapes you can use either three of four pillars. Either method holds the weight of the tier above and it is a matter of deciding which you think looks better.

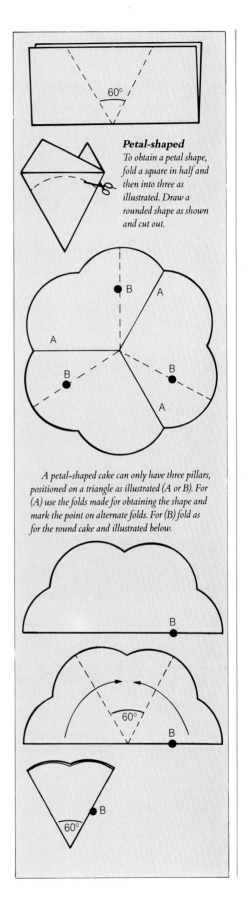

Round

To obtain a round shape, fold a square into four, draw a quarter-circle shape and cut out.

A round cake can either have four pillars on the cross (A) or three pillars on the triangle (B). For the cross, fold into four, open and mark points (A) on the folds. For the triangle, fold as illustrated: fold in half and mark the first position (B) the correct distance from the centre of the cake according to the chart on page 128; fold into three making an angle of 60 degrees, and mark the second position (B) on the outside fold; open up and mark the third point (B) on the third fold.

Square

A square cake can have 4 pillars either on the cross (A) or on the diagonal (B). For the cross, fold the template into four, open up and mark points (A) on the folds. For the diagonal, fold the square into four and then in half diagonally. Open up and mark points (B) on the diagonal folds.

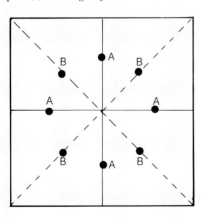

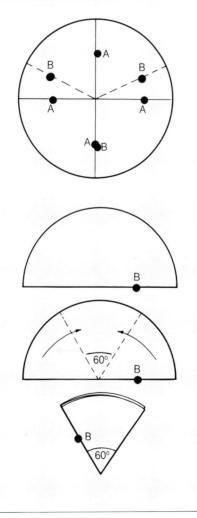

Petal-shaped
To obtain a petal shape, fold a square in half and then into three as illustrated. Draw a rounded shape as shown and cut out.

A petal-shaped cake can only have three pillars, positioned on a triangle as illustrated (A or B). For (A) use the folds made for obtaining the shape and mark the point on alternate folds. For (B) fold as for the round cake and illustrated below.

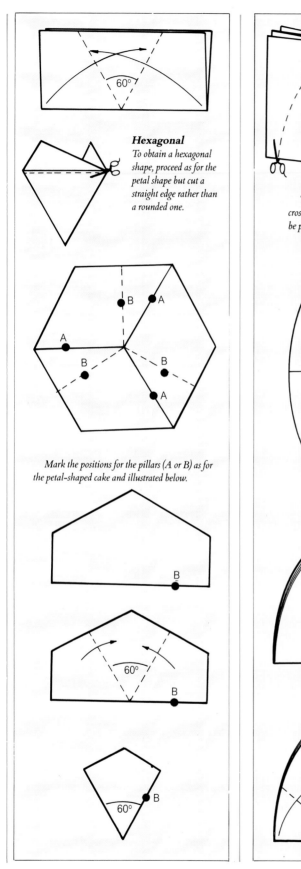

Hexagonal

To obtain a hexagonal shape, proceed as for the petal shape but cut a straight edge rather than a rounded one.

Mark the positions for the pillars (A or B) as for the petal-shaped cake and illustrated below.

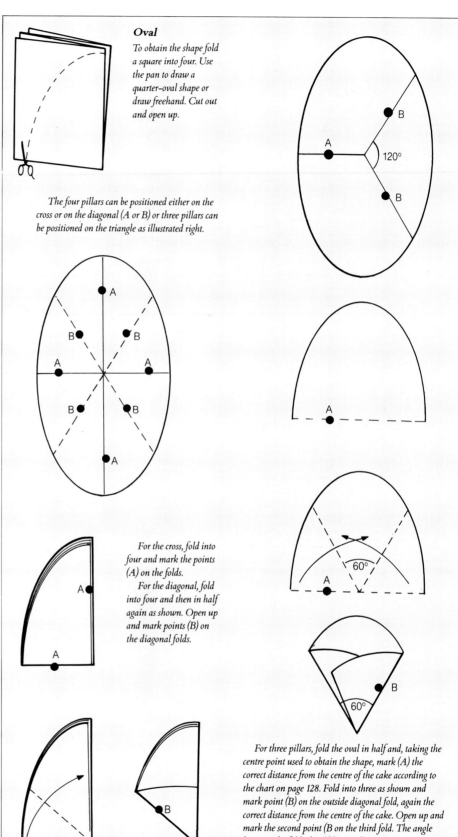

Oval

To obtain the shape fold a square into four. Use the pan to draw a quarter-oval shape or draw freehand. Cut out and open up.

The four pillars can be positioned either on the cross or on the diagonal (A or B) or three pillars can be positioned on the triangle as illustrated right.

For the cross, fold into four and mark the points (A) on the folds.

For the diagonal, fold into four and then in half again as shown. Open up and mark points (B) on the diagonal folds.

For three pillars, fold the oval in half and, taking the centre point used to obtain the shape, mark (A) the correct distance from the centre of the cake according to the chart on page 128. Fold into three as shown and mark point (B) on the outside diagonal fold, again the correct distance from the centre of the cake. Open up and mark the second point (B on the third fold. The angle between the folds should be 120 degrees.

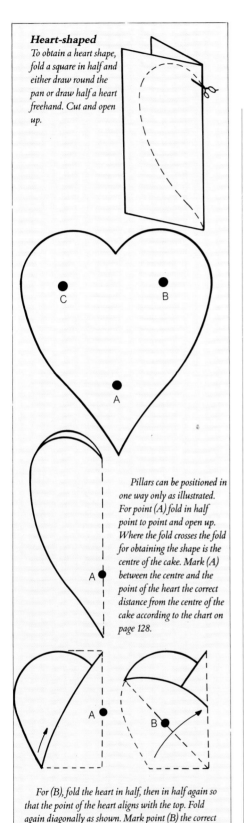

Heart-shaped
To obtain a heart shape, fold a square in half and either draw round the pan or draw half a heart freehand. Cut and open up.

Pillars can be positioned in one way only as illustrated. For point (A) fold in half point to point and open up. Where the fold crosses the fold for obtaining the shape is the centre of the cake. Mark (A) between the centre and the point of the heart the correct distance from the centre of the cake according to the chart on page 128.

For (B), fold the heart in half, then in half again so that the point of the heart aligns with the top. Fold again diagonally as shown. Mark point (B) the correct distance from the centre of the cake. Open up the heart and mark point (C) in a position corresponding to point (B).

ASSEMBLING TIERS

It is very important for the stability of the finally assembled cake that the tiers are level. To ensure this, position the pillars on the cake and check whether the tops are horizontal with a spirit level.

1 Work out the position of the pillars on the template according to the instructions on page 28. Put the template on the cake and to mark where the pillars are to be positioned. Remove the template.

2 The weight of the upper tiers is supported on wooden skewers.

3 Place a wooden ruler or straight edge on top of the pillars and hold a skewer vertically alongside the cake with the tip of the skewer resting on top of the cake board. This way the measurements include the depth of the cake, the height of the pillars and the thickness of the ruler or straight edge.

4 Mark the skewer with a pencil where it meets the top of the straight edge. This ensures that the approximate 2mm/⅛in thickness of the ruler or straight edge is the amount of the skewer which will protrude from the top of the pillar. The skewer for each cake should be marked and cut to the same length.

5 To insert the skewers into the cakes, carefully push them into the icing, marzipan and cake until the point of the skewer reaches the cake board.

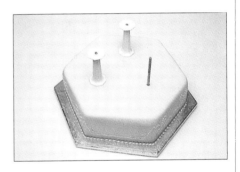

6 Drop the pillar down over the skewer. It is important to ensure that the tops of the skewers are horizontal in relation to each other.

7 Repeat the procedure for each cake. When you are storing the cakes, while you are working on them and when they are finished, do not put them in airtight containers or in a cold cupboard or refrigerator. Keep them at room temperature in cardboard boxes.

NOTES

Cutting the cake

Wedding cake is traditionally served in 2.5cm/1in square pieces, or 6cm/2½in slices. The information in this table will help you calculate what size cake to make based on the number of guests invited. Do not forget extra pieces to send to absent friends and relatives.

Avoiding waste

There is much less wastage if a cake is cut in slices as illustrated, rather than in wedges.

Size of cake	No of slices (fruit cake)	No of slices (sponge cake)
12.5cm/5in round	14	7
12.5cm/5in square	16	8
15cm/6in round	22	11
15cm/6in round	27	14
18cm/7in round	30	15
18cm/7in square	40	20
20cm/8in round	40	20
20cm/8in square	54	27
23cm/9in round	54	27
23cm/9in square	70	35
25cm/10in round	68	34
25cm/10in square	90	45
28cm/11in round	86	43
28cm/11in round	112	56
30cm/12in round	100	50
30cm/12in round	134	67

British/American terms

The list below gives some American equivalents or substitutes for the terms and ingredients used in this book.

Ingredients	
British	**American**
almonds, flaked	almonds, slivered
bicarbonate of soda	baking soda
bilberries	blueberries
biscuits	cookies
cocktail stick	toothpick
coconut, disiccated	coconut, shredded
cornflour	cornstarch
crystallized fruit	candied fruit
chocolate caraque	chocolate curls
chocolate, plain	chocolate, semi-sweet
cream, double	cream, heavy, or use whipping cream
cream, single	cream, light
cream, sour	cream, dairy sour cream
digestive biscuit crumbs	graham cracker crumbs
essence	extract
flour, plain	flour, all-purpose
flour, self-raising	flour, self-raising
gelatine	gelatin
glacé cherries	candied cherries
golden syrup	light corn syrup
greaseproof paper	parchment paper
marzipan	almond paste
nutmeg, grated	nutmeg, ground
sugar, caster	sugar, superfine
sugar, demerara	sugar, light brown granulated
sugar, icing	sugar, confectioners'
sultanas	golden raisins, or seedless white raisins
top of milk	half-and-half
treacle	molasses
white fat	shortening

Equipment and terms	
aluminium foil	aluminium foil
baking sheet	cookie sheet
biscuit cutters	cookie cutters
cake tin	cake pan
swiss roll	jelly roll

Tip conversions

BEKENAL*	WILTON
Plain Round 00, 0, 1, 2, 3, 4	**Round** 000, 00, 0, 1in (long tips) 2 to 9 (intermediate round)
Rope 42, 43, 44, 52	**Stellar** 501, 502, 504, 172
Star 5, 7, 9, 11, 12, 13, 15	**Open Star** 13 to 35
Petal 57, 58, 59	**Rose and Petal** 362, 363, or 101, 102, 103
Basket 22	**Basket and Ribbon** 47, 48, 49
Forget-me-not 37	**Drop Flower** 224, 225, or 108, 109

* Bekenal tips are used throughout the book and are considered amongst cake decorators to be about the best in the world. This chart contains the Wilton equivalents — some correspond exactly but for others there are no exact substitutes.

A note on measures

The recipes in this book give quantities in metric, imperial and American measures The metric measures are based on the standard 25g = 1oz and 600ml = 1 pint units. The American measures are based on the standard 8oz cup measure (solids and liquids).

Spoon measures are level unless otherwise stated and are based on the British Standard teaspoon and tablespoon. If you have a set of metric measuring spoons, the equivalents are 5ml = 1 teaspoon and 15ml = 1 tablespoon.

Each set of measures in the recipes has been calculated separately, so remember to follow only one set as the measures are not interchangeable.

TRACE-OFF
TEMPLATES

The shapes shown on the following pages are
ready to trace-off for run-out designs. Use
greaseproof or waxed paper and trace round
the individual outlines with a thick pencil.
Use as described on pages 126-7.

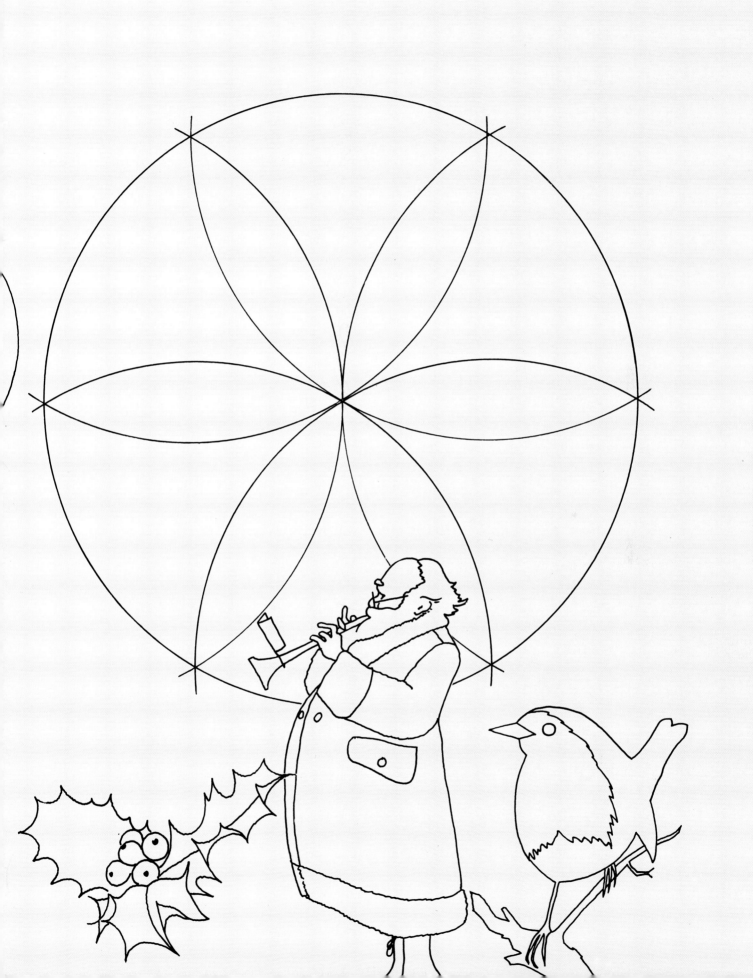

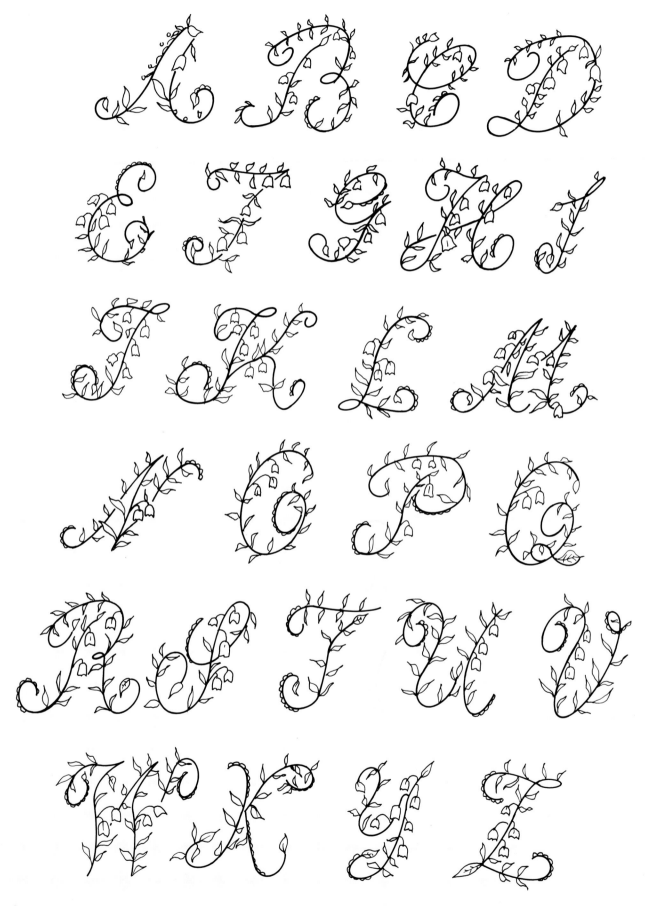

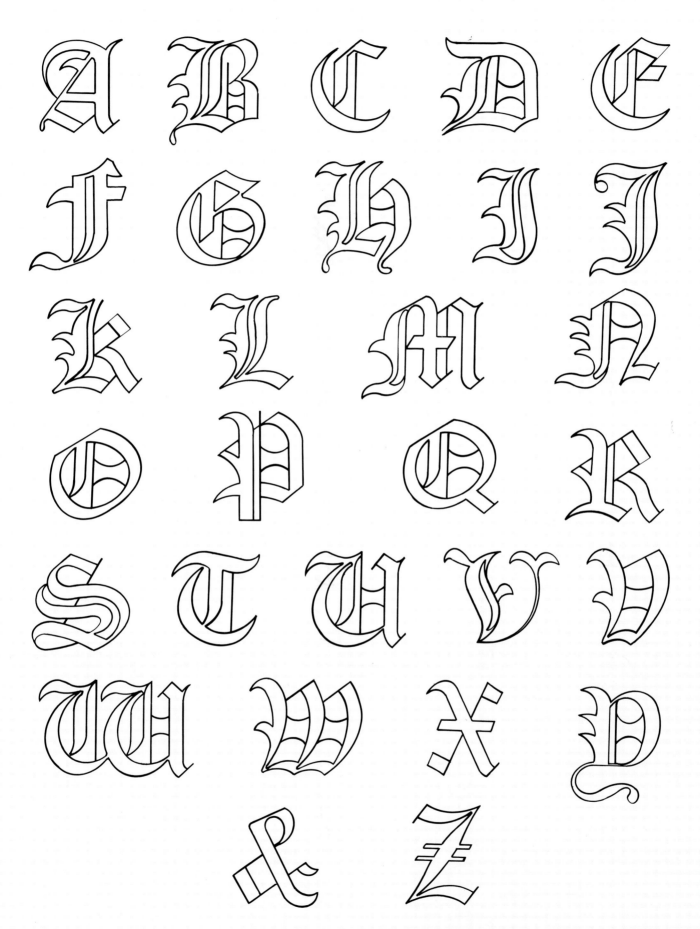

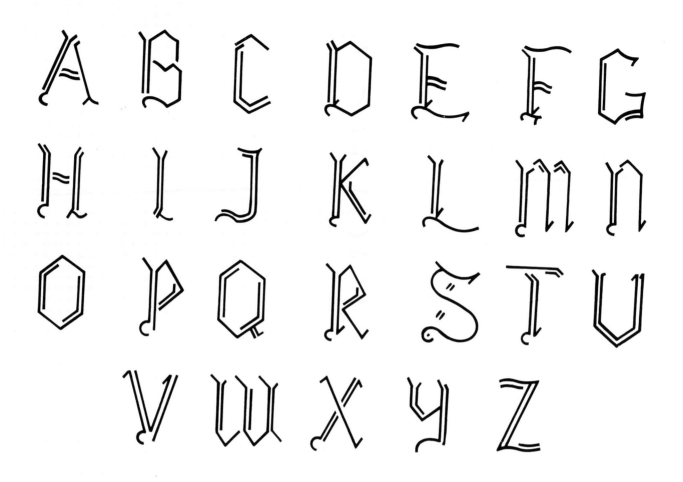

1 2 3 4 5
6 7 8 9 0

1 2 3 4 5 7 8
3 6 9 0

1234567890

1234567890

1234567890

INDEX

Figures in *italics* refer to corresponding picture captions.
Figures in **bold** refer to corresponding recipes.

ACKNOWLEDGEMENTS

The following cakes were designed and demonstrated by
Woodnutt's of Hove, Sussex: pages 7, 22, 26, 27, 30, 31, 39, 53, 54,
55, 56, 57, 58, 59, 66, 67, 68, 69, 70, 71, 74, 75, 78, 79, 84, 85, 98, 99,
103, 112, 113, 114, 115, 116, 117, 121, 123, 124, 125, and 131.

Thanks also to G. T. Culpitt Limited, Hatfield, and the Reject
Shop, Beauchamp Place, London for their assistance.